MODERN WORLD NATIONS

India

Douglas A. Phillips

and

Charles F. Gritzner

South Dakota State University

CHELSEA HOUSE
PUBLISHERS
A Haights Cross Communications Company

Philadelphia

Frontispiece: Flag of India

Cover: Ghats in Varanasi.

CHELSEA HOUSE PUBLISHERS

VP, NEW PRODUCT DEVELOPMENT Sally Cheney
DIRECTOR OF PRODUCTION Kim Shinners
CREATIVE MANAGER Takeshi Takahashi
MANUFACTURING MANAGER Diann Grasse

Staff for INDIA

EXECUTIVE EDITOR Lee Marcott
PRODUCTION EDITOR Jaimie Winkler
PICTURE RESEARCH 21st Century Publishing and Communications, Inc.
COVER DESIGNER Keith Trego, SERIES DESIGNER Takeshi Takahashi
LAYOUT 21st Century Publishing and Communications, Inc.

A Haights Cross Communications Company

http://www.chelseahouse.com

First Printing

1 3 5 7 9 8 6 4 2

Library of Congress Cataloging-in-Publication Data

Phillips, Douglas A.
    India / Douglas A. Phillips and Charles F. Gritzner.
       p. cm.—(Modern world nations)
Includes index.
Contents: Introducing India—Physical environment—Early India—From the era of
European dominance to independence—Cultures of India—Government—India's
economy—Cities in India—India looks ahead.
    ISBN 0-7910-7237-1 HC   0-7910-7503-6 PB
    1. India—Juvenile literature. [1. India.] I. Gritzner, Charles F. II. Title. III Series.
DS407 .P46 2002
954—dc21
                                                                    2002015807

Table of Contents

MODERN WORLD NATIONS

India

Despite its size and population, India remains a mystery to most Westerners. Its people, numbering just over one billion, reflect the country's rich history and diverse cultural and religious customs.

Introducing India

D o you enjoy mysteries? If you do, you will love India, a country shrouded in mystery to most people throughout the Western world today. To most of us, India is a little-known, somewhat mysterious, quite confusing, and yet exotic distant place. It remains little known simply because most people in the West rarely study, read much about, or travel to this vibrant nation. India is very complex. Its religions, politics, economy, history, society and culture, and huge population present a kaleidoscopic array of cultural practices and conditions. The diversity and complexity can be quite confusing to anyone who does not know this distant land and its peoples. India is much like an onion. Onions come in many different colors and can vary greatly in taste. Peeling off one layer only reveals another layer underneath. India, like an onion, also has many varieties and layers.

Jutting southward into the Indian Ocean, India is a large triangle-shaped nation. Its 1,229,737-square-mile (3,287,590-square-kilometer) area makes it the world's seventh-largest state, yet it only covers an area roughly the size of the United States east of the Mississippi River. Because of its size, diversity, location, and its isolation from the remainder of Asia, India is often referred to as a subcontinent. Although it is not as large as a continent, the country has many unique characteristics. India is tremendously diverse in its terrain, which ranges from the towering, snow-capped Himalayas in the north—the world's highest mountain range—to the table-flat plains of the Ganges Plain and Punjab. Climate ranges from parched desert in the northwest to dense rain forest in the remote far eastern part of the country. The famous monsoon drenches the subcontinent during one season, and leaves it bone-dry the next.

Even though India has a relatively large land area, the country is very densely populated. With just over one billion people (1,045,000,000, July 2002 estimate), India ranks second, behind China, in population. In fact, one of every seven people on the planet is Indian. With nearly 820 people crowded into each square mile (2,124 per square kilometer), India's population density is ten times greater than that of the United States. Since much of the land in India is too mountainous, too dry, or too wet and heavily forested for productive settlement, the actual population density is much greater in habitable areas.

India's population not only is huge, it also is growing very rapidly. With a 1.7 percent annual increase, 17 million new people are added to the country's population each year—nearly as many as live in New York, the second most populated state in the United States. At the present rate of growth, India's population will double in 39 years. If this rate continues, within several decades the country will pass China to become the world's most populated land. India has 50 million more people under the age of 14 than the entire population of the United States. They soon will reach the age when they will begin raising families. Providing space, resources, and economic opportunity for a rapidly growing population is one of India's greatest challenges.

Having such a huge population presents India with both challenges and opportunities. India is a very rural country. Nearly 75 percent of its people live in rural areas, most often in villages where they engage in traditional types of farming to meet their family needs. Providing food, clothing, and shelter to over a billion people is a staggering task. Religion is very important to most Indians, yet this part of the world has a long history of religious conflicts. Muslims and Hindus have clashed frequently over the years and many other religions add to the complexity of developing a spirit of cooperation in such a diverse nation. Even with these challenges, India can boast about many things. It is the birthplace of Hinduism and Buddhism, two of the world's great religions. The country has a strong democratic system of government. Increasingly, its population is educated, and many Indians are making important contributions to science, technology, and the arts. India also recently became a member of the elite club of countries possessing nuclear weapons.

The name India comes from *Indos*, which refers to the Indus River. Although the Indus River valley is now mostly located in Pakistan, the river's source is in India near the city of Srinigar. It was here that India's first civilization—The Indus River Civilization—attained a high level of cultural development. Its roots have been traced to as early as 2500 B.C., and it existed for over 1,000 years. Even earlier traces of human activity have been identified in the Indus Valley. Evidence has been found of Early Stone Age people who roamed this land some 500,000 years ago.

Before independence in 1948, India was a British colony. Its land area was greater at that time as it had, in addition to its present territory and borders, all of the land now belonging to the neighboring countries of Pakistan and Bangladesh.

India is located in south central Asia. It is bordered by Pakistan to the west, Nepal and Bhutan on the north, China to the northeast, and Bangladesh and Myanmar on the east. The island country of Sri Lanka is located about 50 miles (80 kilometers) south of India. This region has not always been friendly or peaceful. India has frequently clashed with China and Pakistan. Disagreements about the ownership of Kashmir, located in northern India, have caused frequent fighting between Pakistan and India. The stakes in this conflict with Pakistan have increased in recent years as both India and Pakistan have successfully tested nuclear weapons. India and China also have had hostile border conflicts that threaten the relationship between the world's two most populated countries.

India has an ancient and highly diverse culture. Religion illustrates this complexity. India is the birthplace and home of Hinduism, the religion practiced today by over 80 percent of the country's population. Buddha became enlightened at the Indian city of Sarnath, and today Buddhism is practiced by many Indians. The country also is home to countless Muslims, Sikhs, Jains, Zoroastrians, Christians, and the members of a number of smaller faiths.

In India, religion plays a very powerful role in people's lives. How would you feel if the way of life you could have was determined by the family that you were born into? What if each day of your life you had to conduct yourself in a manner that was defined by this set role? In other words, if the life you were born into allowed very few choices? What you did, who you married, where you lived, and all the many things that you

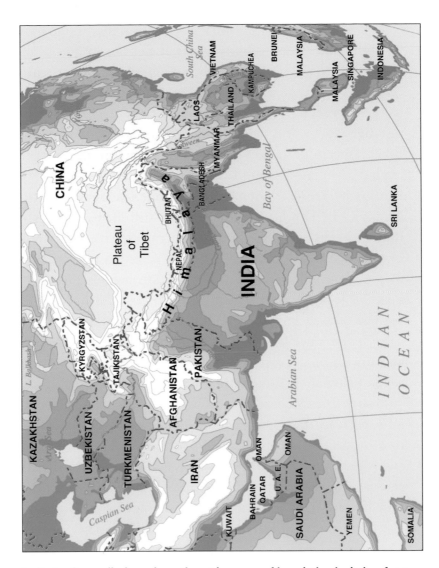

India is often called a subcontinent because of its relative isolation from the remainder of Asia. The country's southern end juts far into the Indian Ocean, with its northern portion sharing borders with Pakistan, China, Nepal, Bhutan, Myanmar, and Bangladesh.

were not allowed to do, were determined even before you were born. Why would people live like this? Hindus choose to live their lives this way because they believe their reward will be to return after death to a better life. For Hindus, this role in life is called a person's *dharma,* or the life goal of fulfilling one's responsibility to his or her family and *caste.* By living in this manner, Hindus believe they will gain religious merit. *Karma* is the Hindu belief that one's status in life is predetermined by one's actions in past lives. How one lives today will determine that future life. These and other aspects of India's various religions will be further explained in later chapters.

Castes are like social classes that are set at birth. Historically, Hindus have been born into a specific caste that they cannot change. Four major castes, with thousands of sub-castes, are recognized. Each caste has its specific duties. Brahmins are the highest caste, whose members become teachers and priests. Kshatryas are the second highest class, forming the rulers and warriors. The third caste is the Vaishyas who served as merchants. The fourth and lowest of the castes, the Shudras, perform the menial work. Below these four castes is another category called the "untouchables." These people hold the most undesirable jobs, such as disposing of the dead, forming cow manure into bricks that are dried and burned as fuel, and clearing away garbage. Untouchables have been discriminated against throughout India's history. The present constitution outlaws discriminatory practices against this group, but tradition is hard to break, particularly in rural villages where many people are uneducated.

India is alive with complexity and diversity. This book will unravel many of the country's mysteries and examine its fascinating cultures. It will trace India's history from the Indus River Civilization to the nuclear age and discuss great leaders like Mohandas K. Gandhi and political dynasties like the House of Nehru. India has many fascinating places, ranging from the beautiful beaches at Kovalam in the south, to the jewel-encrusted Taj Mahal in Agra, and to the majestic snow-capped Himalayas in the north. The physical geography, government, and economy of the country also are included in this story, as is a glance at the challenges and opportunities facing India and its people in the future.

India has towering mountain ranges, such as the Himalayas seen here, parched deserts, tropical rain forests, and broad wetlands. The often extreme climate includes devastating droughts and torrential floods that have tested her people's ability to adapt and thrive.

2

Physical Environment

"**M**ore than 1,000 killed in India as temperatures soar to 122°." "Floods kill thousands and leave millions homeless." "Severe drought affects millions in parched India." "Thousands at risk of Himalaya glacier floods." "20,000 killed and 500,000 homeless as devastating quake strikes India." "Raging elephant kills 12 people." These headlines from recent years are typical of those that could appear at any time in India. Nearly all of the country's 100 million people live very close to nature. As a dominantly rural, agrarian population, India's people depend upon land, soil, rain, and sun for their survival. But, all too frequently, nature takes a heavy toll on the land and people.

Nature has endowed India with many extremes. The world's

highest and largest mountain range looks down on vast low-land river plains. Lifeless desert landscapes stand in marked contrast to dense tropical rain forests. Northeastern India is one of the earth's wettest places, whereas northwestern India is one of the driest. In this monsoon-influenced part of the world, even the seasons offer sharp contrast with six months of extreme wet followed by six months of extreme dry.

INDIA AS PART OF THE INDIAN SUBCONTINENT

India with its four neighbors, Pakistan, Bangladesh, Nepal, and Bhutan are often referred to as the subcontinent of Asia. Although there is no physical division between this region and the rest of the Asia landmass, referring to it as a separate place is understandable. In particular, India's culture, or the way of life of its people, differs greatly from that of its neighbors. In order to fully appreciate how these sharp differences arose, one must look to the region's physical environment.

Cultural geographers recognize that physical isolation from outside ideas and other influences plays a very important role in cultural development. Simply stated, people who live in areas of easy access tend to change their ways of living much more rapidly than do people who live in remote areas with poor access. India's relative isolation has made it possible for the country to develop and maintain its own distinctive culture. No railroads link the subcontinent with the outer world. Few roads reach beyond its borders. As you will learn in Chapters 3 and 4, over the centuries India has been subject to occasional invasions of foreign influence, each of which has left a small imprint on Indian culture. However, India has been able to absorb these outside influences and maintain its own strong cultural identity.

To the north, the world's highest mountain barrier, the towering Himalayas, form an almost insurmountable wall between India and China. To the west, India is separated from Southwest Asia by north–south trending mountain ranges and vast expanses of parched desert. Between India and the exotic cultures of Southeast Asia lie steaming rain forests and a series of north–south trending jungle-clad mountains.

Even the seasonal winds sweeping across the Indian Ocean to the country's shores have helped it remain isolated. Until the seventeenth century, when developments in sails and shipbuilding made it possible to sail into the wind, vessels could only sail in any given direction for roughly six months. Physical barriers and the cultural isolation they made possible, do, in a sense, lend strength to the idea of an Indian subcontinent.

THE LAND

India's land features can be divided into three general regions. First, there are the Himalaya and associated mountain ranges along the northern border. Second, there are the uplands of peninsular India dominated by the Deccan Plateau and associated hills. The third region consists of the lowland plains formed by the Ganges River, and locally by headwaters of the Indus River in the northwest and Brahamaputra River in the east.

Imagine a bulldozer pushing a huge pile of dirt and rock. In a sense, this is how the Himalaya range was formed. India occupies a northward-moving tectonic plate. Millions of years ago, this plate began to slam into southern Asia, creating the tectonic (mountain-building) forces that created the world's highest and largest range of mountains. That process continues today, resulting in continued mountain-building and the many earthquakes that rock the region.

Mountains

The Himalaya and associated ranges form India's roughly 1,000-mile- (1610-kilometer-) long northern border with

China. Tucked away in the range are several small political units: independent Nepal, Indian protectorate Bhutan, and small Sikkim (which became an Indian state in 1975), and Kashmir (claimed by both India and Pakistan). More than 100 Himalayan peaks reach above 24,000 feet (7,315 meters). (By contrast, the highest peak in the Western Hemisphere is South America's Mt. Aconcagua at 22,831 feet, or 6,806 meters.) India's highest mountain is Kanchenjunga, which rises to 28,208 feet (8,598 meters) along its border with eastern Nepal. (The highest peak in the world—Mt. Everest—is on the border between China and Nepal and is 29,028 feet, or 8,848 meters.)

For a stretch of more than 1,000 miles (1,610 kilometers), no road passes across the Himalaya, making it one of the earth's greatest barriers and most inaccessible areas.

Peninsula and Plateau

Much of peninsular India is upland terrain bordered on both margins by narrow coastal plains. The dominant feature of this region is the lava-formed Deccan Plateau. The plateau surface generally decreases in elevation from west to east. Several low mountain ranges and widely scattered hills rise above the plateau surface, contributing to the region's generally rugged plateau terrain. Streams flowing from the western highlands eastward to the Bay of Bengal have eroded and deeply divided the plateau's surface into hills and ridges, further adding to the ruggedness of the land. The plateau is bordered by mountains called the Western Ghats and Eastern Ghats. Technically, the Ghats are not really mountains. They are hardly noticeable when viewed from the upland plateau. When the plateau's escarpments (steep edges) are seen from the bordering low-lying coastal plains, however, they do appear as mountains. Narrow ribbons of fertile coastal plain—the Malabar Coast in the west and Coromandel

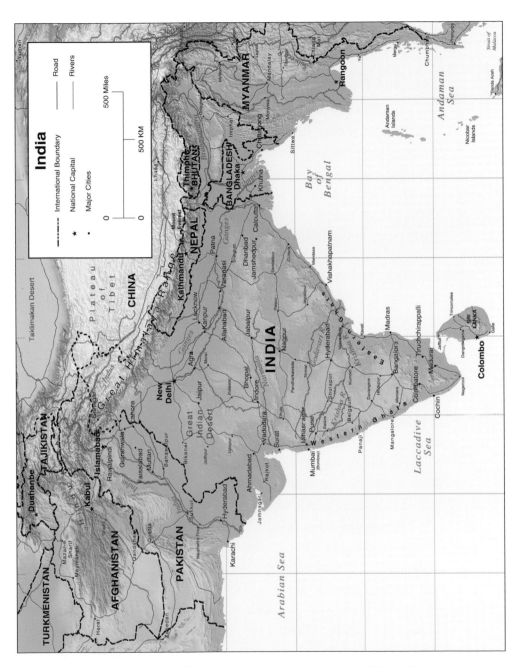

As this map shows, India's northern border is a natural boundary formed by the great Himalayan ridge. For a distance of over 1,000 miles, no roads cross these vast mountains, isolating India from a large part of Asia.

Coast in the east—occupy the areas between the Ghats and the Arabian Sea and Bay of Bengal.

Lowland Plains

India's fertile lowland plains are a gift of three great rivers—the Indus, Brahmaputra, and Ganges. The Indus River, which forms the oasis core of neighboring Pakistan, actually is fed by headwaters that begin in India and Kashmir. As the streams cascade from the mountains to the lowland plain below, they deposit fertile alluvium (stream-deposited silt). Here, in the Indian region called Punjab ("five rivers"), is the country's major area of irrigated agriculture and the growing of wheat and cotton. Farther to the south, bordering Pakistan and distant from life-giving streams, the plain continues as the nearly lifeless Great Indian Desert (also called the Thar Desert).

Much of northeastern India is a very low, moist, tropical area formed by the floodplain of the Brahmaputra. This huge river begins in the snow- and ice-covered highlands of Tibet. It flows eastward for some 500 miles (805 kilometers) until it snakes its way through a huge gorge, turns southward, and plunges thousands of feet to the lowland plains of India's Assam region. The Brahmaputra then flows westward and passes into Bangladesh where it joins the Ganges.

The Ganges River forms India's heartland. The mighty artery is at once sacred, romantic, mystical, and highly polluted, yet it plays a vital role in the daily lives of tens of millions of Indian people. Along its almost 1,500-mile (2,415-kilometer) course and across its 450,000 square miles (1,165,000 square kilometers) of drainage basin, can be found most of India's population settlement, agricultural production, industry and commerce, transportation network, and history.

The plain formed by the Ganges is one of the flattest and most fertile areas on Earth. Over millions of years, the river has deposited silt to depths measured in miles. No stones litter its surface and hardly a hill or mound of earth can be found anywhere. In the last 1,000 miles (1,610 kilometers) of its course, the Ganges drops only 500 feet (152 meters) in elevation. Few rivers can match the importance that the Ganges holds for India and its teeming masses.

WEATHER AND CLIMATE

When one thinks about India's weather and climate, the word monsoon immediately comes to mind. Nowhere else on earth are so many people as dependent upon a seasonal weather event. But the country's variety of weather offers much more than just the monsoon. India lies between nine and thirty-five degrees north latitude, placing most of the country in the tropics or subtropics. Elevation and other factors affecting temperature and precipitation, however, combine to give India a great variety of conditions.

To the west, bordering Pakistan, the Great Indian Desert sprawls across an area nearly the size of Texas. It is a land of far too little water. Annual rainfall amounts to no more than four inches (100 millimeters) in drier parts of the desert. With searing hot summer temperatures often far exceeding 100°F (38°C), potential water loss through evaporation is at least ten times that amount. Much of the desert is covered with shifting sand dunes interspersed with gravel plains and rock outcrops. Within the desert core area, there are no oases. Under these conditions, vast expanses are nearly empty of plant life, with no cacti, palms, or other large plants breaking the bleak and monotonous landscape.

Eastern India's Assam State is a land of too much water. Here are found the steaming tropical swamps and marshes of the Brahmaputra floodplain. Aside from the river's occasional flooding, other water troubles exist in Assam and its neighboring state, Meghalaya. Since 1861, the town of

Cherrapunji, located at an elevation of 4,500 feet (1,377 meters) in the Khasi Hills, holds the dubious distinction of having received the world record amount of precipitation in one year—more than 900 inches (22,860 millimeters). That is 75 feet (23 meters) of rain! Cherrapunji and neighboring Mawsynram both receive an average of 420–430 inches (10,668–10,992 millimeters) of precipitation annually, making them the world's second wettest spots. Mt. Wailaleale, on the Hawaiian island of Kauai, receives 460 inches (11,684 millimeters) of rain a year. What makes eastern India's condition so unique is that during six months of each year, Cherrapunji and Mawsyrnam, as well as the rest of this extremely wet region, suffers often severe drought conditions. To understand how this can happen, one must understand the key element of India's weather—the famous monsoons.

Monsoons

Monsoon is derived from the Arabic word *mausim*, which means "season." The term originally was used by Arab mariners in reference to the seasonal shifting of winds in the Indian Ocean. During the summer season, winds generally blow northward over the hot, tropical waters of the Indian Ocean until reaching land. Saturated with moisture, they bring torrential rains to much of India. During the winter months, wind direction reverses, blowing southward from dry interior Asia. Months may pass without a cloud in the sky. In the absence of cloud cover, temperatures rise. Even in the winter, most of India experiences warm tropical or subtropical temperatures. But plant life becomes dormant, crops shrivel, livestock suffer, and many streams, ponds, and wells become dry.

Before the onset of the monsoon, conditions can become unbearable. In May of 2002, a heat wave gripped southeastern India bringing scorching temperatures that reached 122°F (50° C). More than 1,000 people died in what was the highest one-week death count on record for any Indian heat wave. According to an Associated Press news report (May 23, 2002), "Tin-roofed shanties turned into ovens, ponds and rivers dried up, birds fell from the sky, and animals collapsed." With conditions such as these, it is little wonder that the annual arrival of the monsoon is eagerly awaited throughout nearly all of India. It can be said that to know India and her peoples, one must know the monsoon.

In his book, *I Shall Not Hear the Nightingale*, Khushwant Singh described the monsoon's arrival and impact:

> Dense masses of dark clouds sweep across the heavens like a celestial army with black banners. The deep roll of thunder sounds like the beating of a billion drums. Crooked shafts of silver zigzag in lightning flashes against the black sky. Then comes the rain itself. First it falls in flat drops; . . . Then it comes in torrents . . . Where there was nothing, there is everything: green grass, snakes, centipedes, worms, and millions of insects.
>
> It is not surprising that much of India's art, music, and literature is concerned with the monsoon . . . Innumerable paintings depict people on roof tops looking eagerly at the dark clouds billowing out from over the horizon. . . An Indian, when the rains come, runs out into the streets shouting with joy and lets himself be soaked to the skin.

ENVIRONMENTAL HAZARDS

In addition to human adjustments necessitated by the monsoon's annual wet and dry cycle, Indians face many other environmental problems. Drought poses a constant threat to people living in all areas of India except, surprisingly, the desert. Deserts, by definition, are places lacking an

India's monsoon rains are world renowned for their ferocity. Although severe, the monsoon season provides welcome rain to farming villages often parched by drought. Here, lightning strikes a television tower during a storm.

adequate water supply. Drought, then, can only occur in locations that normally have adequate water. The primary cause of drought in India is the late onset of the monsoon, or a weakened monsoon season bringing less rain to the region. Geographer George B. Cressey noted in *Asia's Lands and*

Peoples, "Life in the subcontinent has always been vitally related to water. Few areas receive the right amount of rain at the right time." With a population now exceeding one billion people, the majority of whom are dependent upon agriculture in a rural setting, a lack of moisture can have catastrophic results. India has built hundreds of dams and thousands of miles of canals to retain water during periods of rainfall and distribute it during periods of need.

Floods also bring devastation to nearly all of India. There are many causes of flooding, each of which is associated with a particular area of the country. Ironically, in the western desert region, flash flooding is one of the leading causes of accidental death and widespread destruction. Runoff from even a small amount of rainfall can gather quickly and form a raging torrent that can destroy everything in its path. Flooding along the lower courses of the Brahmaputra and Ganges rivers is becoming increasingly common and has devastating effects. Monsoon rains swell the mighty rivers and their tributaries that flow from the Himalayas. Human activity, not increased rainfall, is the primary cause of these floods. Mountainsides are being stripped of their woodlands in response to the needs of a growing population. Rainwater gathers quickly and rushes down the cleared slopes into tributary streams, rather than seeping into the soil, or reaching streams slowly.

Cyclones (the name for hurricanes or typhoons in the Indian Ocean) also can bring devastation to low-lying areas of India bordering the Bay of Bengal. Torrential rains often accompany cyclones, but the greatest danger is from wind-driven storm tides. In 1970, a 20-foot surge of water, pushed by winds of 150 miles per hour (241 kilometers per hour), swamped the delta region, part of which is in Bangladesh. Five hundred thousand people may have perished, making the event the worst natural disaster in recorded history. In 2002, the United Nations Environment Program (UNEP) announced what it believes to be still another flood threat. Temperatures in the Himalayas have risen by some 2°F during the past 30 years. As a result, many lakes that are fed by glacial meltwater are filling beyond capacity. According to UNEP estimates, more than 40 Himalayan lakes could overflow or burst their banks, sending millions of gallons of floodwater churning into valleys below, placing the lives, land, and homes of several million people in jeopardy.

Because India occupies an active tectonic plate, approximately 60 percent of the country is subject to earthquake activity. During the past two centuries, at least 20 quakes have occurred that measured 6.0 or higher on the Richter Scale, which is a measure of earthquake intensity. Many of these events have brought widespread death and destruction. Of India's densely populated areas, the west is most vulnerable. In 1993, a quake rocked an area near Mumbai (Bombay) killing some 10,000 people. The country's most devastating earthquake occurred in late January 2001 in Bhuj, a city in Gujarat State, west of Ahmadabad. The tremor measured 7.6, ranking it as one of the most severe quakes ever. Official government figures placed the death toll at just under 20,000 and the number of injured at 166,000. Some 600,000 people were left homeless with 348,000 houses destroyed and another 845,000 severely damaged. More than 20,000 cattle were killed and estimates of economic loss reached as high as US$5 billion.

Wildlife in various forms also pose a hazard in India. The deadly cobra is one of several dozen poisonous snakes. Elephants and tigers attract tourists, but also can turn deadly, attacking animals and people alike. Rats and mice destroy tons of food and create a menace to health wherever they are found. Many insects transmit diseases and microorganisms cause a variety of maladies including dysentery, a major cause of death. Because of Hindu religious beliefs, no form of life is killed.

India's natural environment is unique in many ways. It offers countless challenges, but it also offers many opportunities. In the following chapters of this book, watch for ways in which people have culturally adapted to, used, been influenced by, or changed the natural environment in which they live and upon which they depend for their survival.

The Lakshmana Temple was constructed in 950 A.D. and is dedicated to the Hindu god Vishnu. The cultural history of India dates back as far as 500,000 B.C., when seminomadic groups of hunter-gatherers lived off the land. From these simple beginnings, India's people have developed rich traditions of art, agriculture, music, and religious worship.

3

Early India

India has a long and exciting history. Its past is filled with heroes and villains, as well as kings, colonial masters, gurus, and religions. Wave after wave of historical events have swept across the land and its people. Each of these historical waves has left elements that contributed to the wealth of culture and traditions that exist today.

In this chapter, India's past is divided into time periods that reflect the major events taking place during that era. When dividing history up into periods, it is important to remember that they do not always have clear beginnings and endings. The events cited also may not immediately affect all of the country. Using time periods does provide a good way for organizing and better understanding the important historical and cultural roots of India.

INDUS VALLEY CIVILIZATION

People have been in India for a very long time. Remains have been found that date as far back as 500,000 B.C. Tools of these early people have been found that point to their hunting and gathering economy. They were seminomadic as they wandered in search of food and other things needed for survival. It was not until much later, perhaps 9,000 to 8,000 B.C., that the dawn of plant and animal domestication in the region made agriculture possible. Eventually societies developed, the first in India being the Indus Valley Civilization. This society was evident from about 2,500 B.C. and existed along the Indus River Valley. Today, the valley is in Pakistan, but this was long before the partition between India and Pakistan. The roots of Hinduism can be traced back to Indus society. Beliefs included some animals holding spiritual powers and the worship of gods. Priests held high places of power and some may have even have ruled the society. Seals have been found in ancient Indus cities that show depictions of their gods and other sacred figures. These findings provide a glimpse at the seeds of Hinduism that were planted during the era of the Indus River Valley Civilization.

Little is known about the Indus Valley Civilization, because the writing has never been deciphered. Most evidence has come from ceramic pottery and other artifacts dating to the period. The community had a strong agricultural component based on wheat and there were great cities like Mohenjo-Daro and Harappa. These were large cities, located over 300 miles (482 kilometers) apart. They were carefully planned, skillfully built, and well organized. It is believed that Mohenjo-Daro had a population of 40,000. Other cities like Lothal, Amri, and Kot Diji were discovered later. All of these findings have revealed a very complex society that existed in this early Indian civilization.

Why did the Indus Valley Civilization decline? There are

different theories on this matter. One theory suggests that there were environmental changes, such as earthquake activity or drought, which may have influenced people to move away from the area. Another belief is that Aryan people moved into the area from the west and began dominating the region. Perhaps, it was a combination of factors. Why the Indus Valley Civilization declined remains a mystery to scientists today.

ARYAN INVASIONS AND THE RISE OF RELIGIONS

The Aryans were from a wide area scattered across Central Asia to Poland. They were not agriculturally based. Rather, they used the power of the horse and chariots to hunt and conquer new lands. They invaded and conquered people in the Middle East, much of Europe, and eventually India starting around 1750 B.C. The horses, chariots, and weapons used by the Aryans provided a tremendous technological advantage over the people of the Indus Civilization who were primarily peaceful farmers. The Aryans were not a homogeneous group and often fought among themselves as well as against others. It is believed they came into India through mountain passes from Afghanistan. They moved slowly into the subcontinent and eventually conquered much of northern India.

The Aryans were avid writers and also brought their religion with them to India. They were responsible for bringing their religious writings, called the Vedas, into India. The Vedas served as the foundation for Hinduism as well as the caste system. It is from the Vedas that priests became entrenched as the highest caste, the Brahmins. This supremacy allowed the priests to gain immense power over daily life. They were able to maintain and extend their power because of the religious teachings in the Vedas. These ideas will be explored more fully in Chapter 5 on Indian culture.

Aryans were meat eaters who raised cattle. This tradition differed from those of earlier peoples in the Indus Valley who were primarily vegetarians. The priests also respected all animal life and advocated vegetarianism. These conflicting practices were the source of some dissension, but eventually they were worked out. The Aryan meat-eating practice partially explains why meat is more commonly eaten today in northern India than elsewhere in the country.

Towards the end of the Aryan period, their lands became fragmented into many small kingdoms and a few republics. Kings ruled the kingdoms, each of which had its own capital city and fertile land area that it controlled. In these rich lands, the kings accumulated great wealth and power because of their landholdings. Only priests had the power to limit the control of the kings. The spiritual authority of the priests gave them tremendous influence both over daily life and over the rituals of the king.

Jainism and Buddhism arose as reactions against some of the teachings of the Vedas. Both of these religious movements rejected the teachings of the Vedas and the unfairness of the caste system with its sharply defined class structure.

The Greek conqueror, Alexander the Great, entered north-western India in 326 B.C. Alexander, king of Macedonia, was a courageous warrior and skilled leader who greatly extended the reach of his empire. He was a visionary who wanted to gain more lands and personal glory. After his long march into India, his troops finally rebelled and refused to go further. His troops were weary after the long travel and constant fighting and they stopped at the Hyphasis (Beas) River. The gains he made in India were never developed and Alexander died in 323 B.C. at the young age of 32.

MAURYAN EMPRE

The Mauryan Empire rose to prominence in 326 B.C. After Alexander the Great, a power vacuum existed in

Northern India. Chandragupta Maurya saw an opportunity to provide new leadership. He had also observed the military strategies of Alexander the Great and applied them to his quest for gaining lands. At 25, he attained power in Magadhan and developed the Mauryan Empire that eventually eradicated the remnants of the Greeks. He established a well-organized government that operated efficiently and eventually controlled much of northern India. Corruption became a problem later in his government and life was very difficult for the common people under Chandragupta's rule. A Brahmin priest served as Chandragupta's primary advisor and exercised tremendous influence over the leader. With his guidance, Chandragupta became very wealthy, but he was disliked and under constant threat of assassination. He felt so threatened that he had servants taste his food in his presence and used spies to uncover plots against him. Chandragupta died in 301 B.C.

Chandragupta's son, Bindusara, ruled for 32 years and extended the Mauryan Empire further into the Deccan Plains and Mysore in the south. His gains consolidated almost all the Indian subcontinent into the empire.

Upon Bindusara's death, his son, Asoka, rose to power in 269 B.C. and ruled for 37 years. He is very famous in Indian history and is fondly thought of for his high moral character. Asoka converted to Buddhism in 262 B.C. This marked a huge personal transformation from being a warrior and king to being a humanitarian. To accomplish this, he set forth rules for righteousness in 14 edicts. The edicts, or rules, were carved on 18 rocks and 30 stone columns that were placed in a number of locations around India. These edicts were the principles Asoka used to place limitations on his powers and to rule his empire. These limitations on the king's power aided the average individual and made Asoka's rule much more humane than that of previous kings. The lions sculpted at the top of some of Asoka's stone columns are still

In 262 B.C., King Asoka of the Mauryan Empire converted to Buddhism. Reflecting this dramatic change from warrior-king to humanitarian, he set forth 14 edicts, placing limitations on his power. Stone pillars like this one proclaimed these new rules and were placed throughout India. Many still stand today.

used by India as national symbols. Today, the lion symbol is found on stamps, coins, and in other places much like the American eagle is used in the United States. Asoka's humanity and benevolent leadership led him to be recognized as one of the noblest leaders ever to rule India. Asoka died in 232 B.C. After his death the Mauryan Empire started to fall apart; it finally collapsed in 184 B.C. splintering into a number of smaller kingdoms.

INDIA'S GOLDEN AGE

After the Mauryan Empire and Asoka's benevolent era of rule, a number of things happened to fragment rule in the region. In eastern and southeastern India, the Andhras rose from an insignificant state to control most of the Deccan Plateau. Under the Andhras, Hinduism continued to flourish. In the north, Mauryans were replaced by the Sungas, who ruled for over 100 years until they were overthrown by the brief Kanvas dynasty. In the north and central regions, Buddhism often competed with Hinduism. Many Buddhist temples and monuments were created during this period. India remained very fragmented during this time up until the fourth century A.D.

In 319 A.D., Chandragupta II established the Gupta Empire. He married the daughter of the important Licchavi family who possessed large areas of land. This strategic political move helped to extend his influence. The Guptas brought renewed attention to Brahmin thinking and values, a factor that helped to cause the decline of Buddhism in India. Hindus adopted Buddha by making him a reincarnation of Vishnu, the Hindu god who was the preserver of the universe and represented mercy. This caused many Buddhists to be brought into Hinduism. The return of Brahmin thinking also meant that the caste system was more important and the untouchables and lower castes became more undesirable. Many of the important seeds of Hindu thinking were sowed during the reign of the Guptas.

Much progress was also made during the Gupta Empire. Sanskrit, the classical language of India, was revived and used in writing. New attention was given to the arts, architecture, mathematics, astronomy, and literature, especially religious literature. The art was expressed in a variety of ways including the impressive work of the religious rock sculpting work done in the caves at Ajanta and Ellora. Many of the greatest examples of Hindu literature were written during the Gupta Empire. The imperial Guptas ruled over northern India until 606 A.D. Although the Gupta Empire was mainly in northern India, it did include a few states in the south. It was never as large as the Mauryan Empire. However the impact of the Gupta Empire greatly affected India's course of history. Because of this rich impact, this era is often referred to as India's Golden Age.

In a repeat of history, the Gupta Empire, much like the earlier Mauryan Empire, broke up into smaller kingdoms. This situation existed until the end of the first millennium when the winds of Islam blowing in from the west became a storm.

ISLAM SWEEPS IN

Muhammad, Islam's prophet from Mecca, died in 632 A.D. Before his death, he had a number of visions that he wrote about in the Koran (Qu'ran). Muslims believe that Muhammad is the prophet of God (Allah), and his writings are the rules for living that must be followed. Followers of Muhammad were uncompromising about their faith and swept east and north to conduct a brutal *jihad*, or holy war, against nonbelievers. In Western Europe, they were stopped in France in 732, but others continued, pushing eastward where there was less resistance. Early invasions into the Indian subcontinent cut into areas of present-day Pakistan.

Their impact was limited, however, and the smaller kingdoms continued to exist up until the early part of the eleventh century.

Starting in 1001, Mahmud of Ghazni conducted a series of violent and destructive raids that drove deep into India. He stole Hindu riches and destroyed many of their temples. Mahmud took the riches from his plundering back home to Ghazni thereby making it one of the greatest Muslim cities of that era. Today, Ghazni is a poverty-stricken town in Afghanistan.

After Mahmud of Ghazni, another wave of Muslim invaders entered India from Turkey through Central Asia. Sultan Muhammad of Ghur led this second wave in 1175. This time the Muslims came to stay, not just to raid and plunder Indian villages and kingdoms. They were also different than earlier non-Muslim invaders like the Huns, who eventually were absorbed into Hindu society and thinking. The second wave of Muhammad's followers did not blend into Indian society. They brought their own religion and did not want to blend Islam into Hinduism, a religion they viewed with contempt. The Muslims' intolerance and contempt for the Hindu faith did not win many Hindu converts, so Hinduism continued to be very strong even with the persecution. The mistrust and hatred between many Hindus and Muslims today has roots reaching far back into the eleventh century.

The first Muslim empire in India was located in the Ganges River Valley. From this base other lands were both conquered and lost. Hindu kingdoms continued to exist in parts of the country, but the Delhi Sultanate (country governed by a sultan) became the most important center of Islamic power in India for most of the time from 1206–1398. Islam continued to be very influential, but was suffering gradual decline until the Mughals arrived and spread their control over India.

THE MUGHAL EMPIRE

The Mughals, like the Aryans, came from Central Asia. *Mughal*, in fact, is the Indian spelling of "Mongol." The era of Mughal power is viewed as the pinnacle of Islamic rule in India. This empire left a rich legacy of contributions to India in elaborate architectural accomplishments, literature, language, and the arts. Under the Mughals most of the Indian subcontinent was unified in a stable political environment.

This wave of Muslims began when Babur left his capital in Kabul, Afghanistan and moved eastward on a mission of conquest. He was a descendent of Genghis Khan and a good military planner. The forces under this Muslim leader conquered the weakened Islamic Delhi Sultanate and then moved southward defeating a strong southern alliance of kingdoms in 1527. Babur died in 1530 with most of northern India under his control. His oldest son, Humayun, followed him on the throne. Humayun's rule was marked by inconsistent military success and administration, as he often went into extended binges of eating, drinking, and using drugs.

Humayun's son Akbar came to the throne at the age of 13. Surprisingly, he turned out to become the most outstanding Mughal leader. Akbar was not only a great military and political genius, but also a supporter of the arts and high culture. His reign provided an era of enlightenment to the empire. Akbar was kinder to the Hindus as he recognized they were needed as a dependable work force. He also knew that their support was necessary for any long-term rule by the Muslims. Thus, some Hindus even served as advisors and bureaucrats in Akbar's government. Greater religious freedom was allowed. He protected Hindu temples and monuments and treated Islam and Hinduism equally. This brought him much greater support from

Hindus than his Muslim predecessors had received. Akbar was also very curious about religions other than Islam. He drew together many of these different ideas and developed his own religion, called the Divine Faith, which took the best aspects of other faiths. Although the Divine Faith did not survive after Akbar's death, his tolerance caused Hindus, Muslims, Christians, Jains, and others to view him favorably. He became a true leader of India, not just a ruling outsider.

Akbar established his capital at Fatehpur Sikri, a location near the city of Agra where the Taj Mahal stands today. Fatehpur Sikri only served as the capital for a few years. Today, Fatehpur Sikri is an abandoned historical site, a virtual ghost town, but its complex of reddish buildings gives the visitor a spectacular glimpse at Akbar's vision.

Other Mughal leaders followed Akbar with the most notable being Shah Jehan and Aurangzeb. Shah Jehan moved the capital from Fatehpur Sikri into Agra and built a new palace called the Red Fort. Shah Jehan is best known for building the Taj Mahal. This spectacular mausoleum was constructed in memory of his favorite wife, Mumtaz Mahal, who died bearing their fourteenth child in 1631. Shah Jehan was devastated by this loss and immediately started construction on this remarkable structure. The Taj Mahal was completed in 1653 and is considered a monument to his love. The dazzling white marble exterior is inlaid with jewels and the symmetry of the building with its four minarets (towers) is unforgettable. Shah Jehan also planned to build an identical black tomb for himself directly across the Yamuna River from the Taj Mahal. His son, Aurangzeb, learned of Jehan's plan and overthrew his father, who then spent the rest of his life imprisoned in the Red Fort with a view of his beautiful Taj Mahal.

Aurangzeb was much less tolerant toward other religions and forced a return to Islam. Many Hindu temples were

The most famous building in India, the Taj Mahal, was built in Agra in 1631 when the Mughal Muslims ruled the country. Shah Jehan ordered construction of this exquisite palace as a monument to his beloved wife Mumtaz Mahal, who died in childbirth.

destroyed under his rule and the people hated him. In contrast to Akbar, both Sikhs and Hindus disliked Aurangzeb. Relationships deteriorated to the point that Sikhs formed military units to protect themselves. Aurangzeb was a good warrior, but he was known to be a liar and was ruthless in exerting his power. During his reign, he extended the Mughal Empire and ruled for 48 years when, to the relief of Hindus and Sikhs, he finally died at the age of 88. By the time of his death, nearly all the Indian subcontinent was under Mughal control. This made it the greatest Indian Empire since Asoka's Mauryan Empire.

After Aurangzeb's death, the Mughal Empire started to decline. Hindu groups like the Rajputs from northern India increased their power and fought against external rulers like the Mughals. In central India, the Marathas had fought against Aurangzeb and continued this struggle after his death. These and other groups from Persia gradually weakened the Mughals until a power vacuum existed. The opportunity was ripe for someone to come and take control. The question was—Who?

In 1765, British governor Robert Clive negotiated a trade agreement from Mughal Emperor Shah Alum.

4

Era of European Dominance to Independence

T he Portuguese were the first western Europeans to arrive in India. They gained a foothold in the rich area of Goa, which they seized in 1510. Under Portuguese control, it became the first Christian colony in India. The Portuguese, however, had limited material and human resources. Their country was not a world power in the same league as the British and the French at that time.

The British first arrived and developed connections with India in 1612. A private group called the East India Company, which was sanctioned by Queen Elizabeth I, made this contact. This company formed trading posts in various cities in India and actually conducted the business of the British for over 250 years. It developed key trading posts in Calcutta, Bombay, and Madras. These cities grew quickly with the trade that strengthened the local economies. The French also had trading posts in India starting in 1674. In Europe, modernize India. By the mid-1850s, the British, who were convinced of their cultural and technical superiority, began to take away local political rule. Using the excuse of mismanagement and poor government, the British believed that their superior form of government should be forced upon these kingdoms. Because of this crackdown, Indians mutinied against British control in 1857.

Many Indians consider this revolt, called the Indian Uprising or Mutiny, the start of the struggle for Indian independence. Many Indians served in the East India Company's army. By 1857 they represented over 90 percent of the British troops in India. In 1857, a new bullet was introduced for use by the troops and rumors quickly spread among the Indian soldiers that these bullets were greased with pig or cow fat. Because bullets were typically held in the mouth before loading, these bullets were considered unusable by Indian troops. Hindus believe that cows are holy and Muslims believe that pigs are unclean. In either case, the bullets were unacceptable. Since the British did not successfully dispel this rumor, the troops rebelled. This mutiny quickly spread across northern India. The British were unable to end the rebellion until the end of 1858.

After that uprising, the British government realized that the East India Company was an ineffective administrator. In the future, India would be ruled directly by the British government. During the second half of the nineteenth century, Indians played a greater role in political processes and some democratic reforms were introduced. The British refrained from meddling with cultural and religious practices. Smaller kingdoms were allowed greater autonomy and suffered less British interference. New treaties were made between the British and the kingdoms that pledged non-interference and guaranteed their boundaries. Partially because of the new hands-off policies, over 500 kingdoms existed in 1900. The British still held control and they supervised the army, but Indians were allowed

The British were quick to impose their cultural standards in India, cracking down on many established cultural practices and building new roads, railways, and a postal system. In 1857, Indians rebelled against their British governors in an uprising that lasted more than a year. Many view this as the first battle for Indian independence.

to hold higher positions in government. The British brought thousands of soldiers from home, thereby creating a larger percentage and presence of British troops in the Indian army.

How long would the people of India tolerate this foreign rule? So many foreigners had ruled India for so long. How would India become its own master? What steps would be taken to secure independence?

STEPS TOWARD INDEPENDENCE

After the Indian Mutiny, many British living in India started to retreat from Indian society. They formed small ethnic enclaves with their own foods, drinks, clothing, sports, leadership made independence a reality by the end of World War II in 1945. During that war, the British put into prison more than 60,000 members of the independence movement, including Congress Party leaders. A short while later, Britain realized it could not sustain the military and political costs necessary to maintain a colonial empire that included control of India. India had created huge political pressures that the British could no longer restrain. Independence was finally realized at midnight on August 14, 1947. Sadly, the celebration was short lived.

INDEPENDENT INDIA

In addition to Mohandas K. Gandhi, two other significant political leaders emerged in India during this time. The first was Jawaharlal Nehru who followed Gandhi as the leader of the Congress Party in 1929. Gandhi was Nehru's mentor and supported Nehru's leadership of the party. The second leader was Muhammad Ali Jinnah. He was a Muslim within the Congress Party who left the party and joined the Muslim League in the 1930s in an effort to protect the interests of Muslims. Muslims were increasingly afraid of being dominated by a Hindu majority. Jinnah recognized this fear and advocated a separate country for Indians who were Muslim. Gandhi and Nehru did not agree with this philosophy. Jinnah continued to build Muslim mistrust and fear of the Congress Party and Hindus. On August 16, 1946, he led a day of direct action to promote having two countries created out of British India. Tragically, the protest turned violent and more than 5,000 Indians were killed in rioting in the city of Calcutta. Reluctantly, Nehru and other leaders agreed that there should be a separate Muslim state to be called Pakistan. Gandhi continued to oppose the separation and was deeply saddened by the reality that had been created. The British representative, Lord Louis Mountbatten, realized that the British could leave India only if two nations were created: India and Pakistan.

In the twentieth century, Mohandas Gandhi emerged as a charismatic leader committed to nonviolent resistance against British rule. Gandhi's work resulted in independence for India in 1947. Here, Gandhi (right) confers with India's first prime minister, Jawaharlal Nehru.

With independence came celebration, then horror. Immediately, Muslims in the new India started fleeing to Pakistan, and Hindus and Sikhs from the new Pakistan fled to India. Thus began the largest short-term human migration in history, with over 17 million people moving in one direction or the other. The migration immediately became violent. People of both religions were persecuted and massacred. Villages on both sides were burned and destroyed. More than one-half million people died, most in the Punjab region.

Gandhi helped to relieve the tension of the mass movements in Bengal. He helped keep Delhi, the Indian capital, as peaceful as possible as Muslims in the city feared persecution by both Hindus and Sikhs. Gandhi conducted a fast until death to try and stop the fighting between Muslims and Hindus in Delhi. His sacrifice accomplished what law enforcement and the armies could not. Hindu persecution of Muslims in Delhi declined. This made some Hindus resent Gandhi; they thought he had protected the Muslims. On January 30, 1948, India and the world were shocked to hear that a Hindu nationalist fanatic had assassinated Gandhi. In response to Gandhi's death, Jawaharlal Nehru, India's first prime minister said, "The light has gone out of our lives and there is darkness everywhere."

In addition to the fighting over Kashmir and Jammu right after independence in 1947, wars between India and Pakistan have occurred in 1965 and 1971. The mistrust between these two powers is still strong today, with each of the countries now having nuclear weapons. Both tested nuclear weapons in 1998. In 1999 they both successfully tested missiles capable of carrying nuclear bombs that threaten each other's security. In 1962, India fought a border war with China, but that situation has been improving in recent years.

Jawaharlal Nehru remained prime minister until his death in 1964. He was the first of his family to rule in what has been called the House of Nehru. He sympathized with India's poor and held Mahatma Gandhi as his mentor. Nehru worked to reduce poverty and the stigma of untouchability. He also placed India on a middle ground during the Cold War, not taking the side of either the United States or the U.S.S.R. With this action, he led the Non-Aligned Movement of countries that remained neutral during the Cold War.

A short time after his death, Nehru's only child, a daughter named Indira Gandhi (no relation to Mohandas K. Gandhi), became head of the Congress Party and prime minister of India. She served as prime minister during most of the years between 1964 and 1984 and her rule was more authoritarian than that of her father. She attempted to crack down on Sikh extremists who had occupied the Sikh's most holy site, the Golden Temple in Amritsar, by sending troops from the Indian Army into the building. In retaliation, her Sikh guards assassinated Indira Gandhi in 1984. That same year, her only living son, Rajiv Gandhi, was selected as prime minister. He served until 1991 when he was murdered during a political campaign. This marked the end of the rule of the House of Nehru for the twentieth century, but their rule after independence is a remarkable era of leadership by one family.

In the 1990s, the Congress Party of Nehru and his family were strongly challenged by coalitions of other parties and by the nationalist Bharatiya Janata Party (BJP). The Hindu-dominated BJP takes a harder stance against Pakistan and is the party that promoted the nuclear tests in 1998. Their political leadership makes Muslims, moderate Indians, and Pakistanis uneasy, as the party is very nationalistic and comes from the roots of the group that assassinated Mohandas K. Gandhi. This nationalistic tendency and the increased number of acts committed by Muslim terrorists in the early twenty-first century continue to threaten the fragile peace existing between India and Pakistan.

Hindus pray in the Ganges River on the first day of the Kumbh Mela festival. India's cultural makeup is indeed diverse. While Hindus comprise a majority of the population (82 percent), the country's religious groups also include Muslims, Christians, Sikhs, Buddhists, Jains, Zoroastrians, and Jews.

5

Cultures of India

A journey though the cultures of India is an exciting and unforgettable trip. It presents a richness of diversity, unlike any other nation, with thousands of cultural variations from those that are presented in this chapter. The foundations of Indian culture have been established over millennia by the introduction of outside influences and the unique mix of Indian religions, languages, castes, and other elements.

RELIGION IN INDIA

A visitor to India is immediately struck by the huge impact of religion on peoples' lives. A person's religion can often be determined simply by his or her appearance, mannerisms, or what he or she eats (or does not eat). Two of the world's great religions were born in India: Hinduism and Buddhism. Other smaller faiths also have roots there. Religious teachers from Buddha to St. Thomas have converted people to their faiths in India, while others have been forced to accept a religion upon threats of pain or death. To unravel the mystery of India, one must examine the religions that provide basic philosophies for life. This chapter examines some of the basic characteristics and beliefs of the major religions in India.

Most Indians are Hindus. Many other religions thrive in the country, however, because India's constitution promises freedom of religion. Even with this freedom, many Indians have suffered religious persecution since independence in 1947. The following chart gives a breakdown of population by religious followers:

POPULATION BY RELIGION		
RELIGION	NUMBER*	PERCENTAGE
Hindu	842,152,502	82.00%
Muslim	123,241,829	12.00%
Christian	24,648,366	2.40%
Sikh	20,540,304	2.00%
Buddhism	7,189,106	0.70%
Jainism	5,135,076	0.50%
Zoroastrianism	102,701	0.01%
Judaism	5,135	0.0005%

*Estimates based on 2001 census data

Hinduism is by far the dominant religion in India today. More than four out of five Indians are Hindus. Muslims are a distant second, as many Muslims migrated to Pakistan during the period of conflict following independence. Other religions include Christianity, Buddhism, Judaism, Jainism, and Zoroastrianism. What do people in these faiths believe? What practices do they observe? These and many other questions will now be examined.

Hinduism

Hinduism is one of the world's oldest religions. It has nearly one billion believers, making it the third-largest religion in the world. India is, by far, the nation with the most practicing Hindus. Hindus believe in a wide variety of gods, which may number from one to over 300 million. Some Hindus believe in all of these gods, while others have a preference for one god. Hinduism is inclusive in that it is open to the ideas of other religions. In fact, it often adopts key individuals and practices from other faiths into the Hindu's belief structure. For example, Buddha, founder of Buddhism, is considered by Hindus to be a reincarnation of Vishnu, the preserver of the universe.

Vishnu is one of the three primary Hindu gods. Some consider him to be much like Jesus Christ in Christianity. The other two are Brahma, the creator, and Siva, the destroyer, who is portrayed as being terrifying in appearance and in actions. Each of these gods endures forever, but may appear to believers in many forms or reincarnations. It is believed that Vishnu will have ten reincarnations and that nine have appeared so far. For example, after Buddha, Rama was the seventh reincarnation of Vishnu and Krishna was the eighth. Each of these reincarnations serves like a mask for God who exists forever, but has many disguises.

Each of these three gods is a male, but each of them has a wife, or a female persona. Parvati is the wife and female aspect of Siva; Lakshmi is Vishnu's wife and the goddess of wealth and prosperity. Brahma's female aspect is called Sarasvati and she is viewed as the goddess of learning.

Many Hindus prefer one of the three main gods to the others. Thus, followers of Vishnu are in a sect called Vaishuavism. Others may follow only Siva, or other gods and goddesses. Some gods, like elephant-headed Ganesh, are worshiped in only certain regions of the country while others, like Vishnu, are worshipped throughout India. Ganesh, God of prosperity and wisdom, was the son of Siva and Parvati and received his elephant head because of the bad temper of his father, Siva. Stories of gods and goddesses abound in Hinduism and make for wonderful conversations and reading.

Some Hindus worship idols. Others do not. Worship is usually private in the home or in a temple. This is unlike Christians, Jews, Muslims, or others who often worship together in congregations. Prayers may be offered to many different gods who can help the Hindu believer solve his or her problems.

Strangely, a person can never "join" the Hindu faith. One must be born into the religion. This is because in the past, one was born into a caste. If one were able to join the faith, how could caste be acquired? If you are born into the Hindu faith, you may practice your religion in a wide number of ways. You can even practice another faith, such as Christianity, and remain within the Hindu faith. This flexibility makes Hinduism unique. Many religions have beliefs or practices attached to them that must be followed.

Reincarnation is another Hindu belief. It is the belief that when a person dies, he or she will be reborn. In Hinduism, the term karma is used to indicate that the things people do in their present life determine what happens in their next life. If they live a good life, according to what is expected, they will return in a better life after reincarnation. Hindus cremate, or burn, the dead, rather than bury them because they believe that the soul will get to heaven more quickly and allow for a quick transition to the next incarnation.

Before death, Hindus believe that there are four stages of life to fulfill one's karma, or destiny. If these steps are fulfilled, a Hindu will be successful in moving through the cycle of life, death, and reincarnation. These four stages of life are:

1. Being a virtuous pure student.
2. Being a married person with a family that, preferably, has many sons.
3. Withdrawing from society to the forest for spiritual meditation and reflection.
4. Becoming a homeless, wandering, self-punishing person awaiting death.

The fourth stage is not required. However, visitors often see Hindus who have sacrificed all of their possessions and attachments, including family, and who have no ties to worldly things. This allows them to properly live the fourth stage, called *samnyasin*.

Hindus also have traditionally believed in the caste system. They believe that a person is born into a *jati*, a predetermined social group or class, that the British called a caste. The caste system was taught by ancient Hindu writings called the Vedas. The Vedas divided Indian society into four castes. The caste system is described in detail later in this chapter.

Islam in India

The second-largest religion in India is Islam, with over 100 million believers. They comprise the nation's largest religious minority and make India one of the most populated Islamic nations. Muslims exert a strong influence on India and have held high government positions, including that of prime minister. In summer 2002, a Muslim scientist, A.P.J. Abdul Kalam, was elected to a five-year term as president.

The prophet Muhammad founded Islam. Basic tenets of the religion are set forth in the Koran, the holiest of all books for Muslims. Muhammad lived in Saudi Arabia in the seventh century. India's Islamic roots started in the eighth century when Arabs started invading northern India. Most of the early

While many Muslims fled to Pakistan following India's independence from Britain, millions remained and formed India's second-largest religious group. Here, Muslim children study at Jama Masjid Mosque in New Delhi.

converts were from the lower classes and some were forced to adopt Islam through threats of death. People who were not Muslim suffered greatly under leaders like Aurangzeb, who led a zealous effort to convert others to Islam. He enforced Islamic beliefs and even destroyed Hindu temples and turned them into mosques. A long line of Muslim leaders continued to carry the religion forward under their rule in parts of the country. Intermarriage, persuasion, higher taxes, and other means were used to convert Hindus to Islam. By the twelfth century, north India was under Muslim control. This control lasted until the eighteenth century.

Muslims believe in one God, Allah, and they believe that Muhammad was his prophet. The Muslim holy day of worship is Friday when they go to the mosque to pray. The rest of the week, prayers are said five times daily. The singing of the call to prayer is an unforgettable experience when visiting an Islamic nation. During prayer, Muslims kneel facing Mecca, Islam's holy city. It is a goal of Muslims to make a pilgrimage to Mecca at least once in their life.

India's Muslims are divided into two major sects, the Shiite and the Sunni. Tensions continue to exist between these two sects in India, as they do in many areas of the world where both religions are practiced.

Some Muslim women still wear the veil, and Muslim men may take up to four wives, as the religion allows polygamy. This practice is mainly found in northern India, where the Muslim population is highly concentrated.

Jainism

There are about five million Jains in India today. Jainism started about 2,500 years ago when a group led by a prophet named Mahavira broke away from Hinduism. He is considered the founder of Jainism. Mahavira and his followers split from Hinduism because they believed that the power of the Hindu priests was too great and that the rituals of the Brahmins were too complicated.

Jains strongly believe in nonviolence. They also believe in *ahimsa,* which means that they respect all life and try, in any way possible, to avoid injuring or killing any living thing. Consequently, Jains are absolute vegetarians. This philosophy even affects their job choice because in many professions, Jains could accidentally kill living things. For example, a farmer could walk in the fields and accidentally step on an insect. For this reason, many Jains work in banking or other businesses where they have become very prosperous and well-respected as community leaders.

Jains live in all parts of India, but are concentrated in the west and southwest. They, like Hindus, also believe in reincarnation. They believe that the universe is infinite. Jainism has two major philosophies in the religion—the Shvetember and the Digamber. Shvetember monks wear white clothes and include women in their sect. Only men can be Digamber monks and they are very austere in their beliefs. For example, they wear no clothes in their temples. In fact, their name, *Digamber*, means "sky clad."

Buddhism

Siddhartha Gautama was born and raised as a prince in a wealthy Indian family. As a youth, he was sheltered in his palace and was not exposed to the outside world, but as a young man, he started traveling outside of the palace. The disease, poverty, and misery he saw in the lives of people outside his sheltered world horrified him. He gave up his wealth and left the palace on a personal search for enlightenment. At first he lived an austere life, eating very little and searching for wisdom. He realized that neither the austere life nor the wealthy one was the true path for enlightenment, so he started advocating the middle path. This path followed a middle route between the extreme of self-indulgence and the extreme of discarding all material things. Using this middle path, he became enlightened at the city of Sarnath. People began calling him *Buddha*, a term meaning "enlightened one" in this area of India.

Buddhism is more of a philosophy and a code of conduct for life, rather than a religion. Buddha believed that the search for material things only caused suffering. This suffering causes people to be reborn again into another life of suffering. Instead, if a person casts out worldly desires, he or she will not need to be born into another life. Buddha taught an Eightfold Path to help his followers control or eliminate their desires in order to reach *nirvana*, which was a state of no suffering. The Eightfold Path instructs followers to believe right, desire right, think right, live right, do the right things, think the right thoughts, behave right, and practice proper deep reflection.

Buddhists believe in nonviolence, but not as strictly as the

Jains. They are vegetarians and many keep statues or pictures of Buddha in their homes. Buddhism became very popular during the Mauryan Empire when Emperor Asoka endorsed it. Later, in India, much of Buddhism was incorporated into Hinduism as Buddha was made a reincarnation of Vishnu. Today there are only about seven million Buddhists in India, but Buddhism remains very popular in China, Japan, Thailand, Cambodia, Myanmar (Burma), and Vietnam.

Christians in India

Christianity has some surprising roots in India. St. Thomas, one of Jesus' disciples, is buried near the city of Madras. He arrived in India in 52 A.D. and preached the teachings of Christianity, far from the source of the faith in what is now Israel. In 1498, Portuguese explorer Vasco da Gama arrived and promoted Christianity in south India. Other Europeans, particularly the Dutch and English, followed with their Christian sects. The Portuguese tried to force their religion upon Indians, but others who followed stressed that becoming a Christian should be voluntary.

Today, Christians in India number about 25 million. They are a majority of the population in two of the smaller states, Mizoram and Nagaland. Christmas and Good Friday are among the Christian holidays celebrated in India.

Many Christian schools have been built in India along with social assistance centers like Mother Teresa's Missionary of Charity, the first of which was started in Calcutta. Mother Teresa, who began her career as a geography teacher, later became world famous for her good works in India and elsewhere in the world. Her initial impact was in India, even though she was born in Skopje, Macedonia.

Zoroastrianism

This religion represents only a small percentage of the population in India, but it is a group that has been very influential.

Followers of Zoroastrianism are called Parsis, because the religion came from Persia around 1,400 years ago. Muslim persecution caused the Parsis to flee from Persia in search of a safe haven in which to practice their faith.

Parsis worship one god, called Ahura Mazda, who is represented as a symbol of fire. Parsis believe that there are both good and bad forces, forces of light and of darkness. The forces of light will overcome those of darkness if people behave properly and do good works. Because of this belief, Parsis are powerful contributors to their communities. For example, Dr. Barucha was a Parsi doctor in Mumbai. In the mid-1950s, he and another doctor started a leprosarium (hospital for those suffering from leprosy). Here, over 200 people were selected each year from the slums of Mumbai to come and receive medical treatment and occupational training free of charge. Patients are allowed to stay up to 2 years while recovering. Dr. Barucha was viewed widely as a powerful force for good within his community.

Parsis also believe that water, air, fire, and the earth are pure and need to be protected. Because of this, they do not cremate or bury their dead. Instead, the dead are placed on platforms on high towers, and vultures and other birds eat the remains. Parsis believe that this method of disposing of the dead does not pollute the soil, air, or water.

Most Parsis in India today live near Mumbai. They play important roles in finance. They also serve as a communications link with Pakistan, hoping to defuse conflict between the two countries. Their numbers are slowly decreasing, because Parsis can only marry other Parsis. Children of mixed religious marriages are not considered Parsis.

Sikhism

Have you ever seen men from India who wear their hair wrapped up in a turban and sometimes have their beards in a net? If so, you may have met a Sikh. Their appearance is based on some of their most basic beliefs and it also helps

The Sikh faith represents a melding of Hindu and Muslim traditions. They embrace both the monotheism of Islam and the Hindu ideas of karma and reincarnation. Persecution of Sikhs by Muslim leaders caused many to become soldiers, and Sikhs still comprise a significant fraction of India's military.

Sikhs recognize others of their faith.

A Hindu named Guru Nanak founded Sikhism in northern India in the fifteenth century. He traveled widely in India and found many ideas of Islam and Hinduism interesting, but they did not reflect what he really believed. He decided to put together the most important and positive ideas from Hinduism and Islam and create a new religion—Sikhism. The Sikhs took many of the ideas from Hinduism, such as reincarnation, karma, and cremation, but they abandoned the caste system. Sikhs, like Muslims, believe in one God and they do not worship idols. The holy book of Sikhs is the Granth Sahib, which includes writings from many early spiritual leaders called *gurus*.

Sikhs believe in equal rights for everyone. They reject the caste system and inequality based on gender, race, religion, culture, or other factors. They do not have priests or clergy, do not believe in fasting, and do not go on pilgrimages. Their most holy place is the Golden Temple in the city of Amritsar, but Sikhs are not required to make a trip there.

Sikhs were persecuted in their early history under various Muslim leaders. Some Guru Sikhs even were put to death. To rise against this tyranny, many Sikhs became warriors. Today, Sikhs are well represented in India's military because of their tradition of military involvement. Even with this military tendency, Sikhs preach understanding and love. A further expression of this is that Sikhism promotes community service and helping the poor.

THE CASTE SYSTEM AND THE UNTOUCHABLES

Old Hindu writings called the Vedas divided society into four social groups or classes that are called *castes,* or *varnas.* People were born into a system that ranked them from highest to lowest caste. The caste into which an individual was born could not change during a person's life. The highest caste described in the Vedas is the Brahmins, who represented the priests and teachers. They traditionally stressed the importance of correct religious practices and would make decisions on religion and caste. The second-highest caste is the Kshatryas, the rulers and warriors. The next caste is the Vaishyas, who represented the merchants and cultivators. The lowest caste is the Shudras, who were farmers and other menial laborers. Many believe that the Brahmins used the caste system to maintain their power and control over others.

Members of the three highest castes are called "twice-born," because of the belief in reincarnation. Vedas believe that a person already has been reincarnated at least once. Within each varna, or caste, there are further subdivisions that reflect more specific information about a person's social status. All of this can make life more complex, especially if a person is trapped in a lower caste. Since people are born into their caste, one's caste is often disclosed by their family name. Mukerjee and Chatterjee, for example, are common names of professors, who are in the Brahmin caste.

Untouchables

The largest minority in India is the untouchables, with more than 160 million people. Untouchables, or *Dalits*, as they are called in India, were outcasts who existed below the four castes. They worked with dirt, leather, the dead, street cleaning, and other difficult and degrading jobs. People in the higher castes could not be touched by, or even fall under the shadow of, an untouchable. If this accidentally happened, the caste member was believed to have been polluted by the untouchable person and would have to be cleansed.

India officially abolished untouchability in Article 17 of the constitution adopted in 1950. The Article states that "Untouchability is abolished and its practice in any form is forbidden." Unfortunately, many problems of discrimination against the Dalits still exist more than a 50 years later, as attempts to remedy the problem have often met resistance. Due to continued Dalit frustration and lingering resistance by some members of higher castes, violence has occasionally occurred between castes and untouchables. Dalits often have turned to self-mutilation, including setting themselves on fire, in their efforts to promote greater equality. The government has worked hard to increase the opportunities for untouchables and other disadvantaged citizens by requiring that companies, universities, and other public institutions set quotas for Dalits, to ensure that some positions are open to them.

Language

India is a country of many tongues. In fact, no other nation of comparable size in the world can match its diversity of over

1,600 different languages still in use today. Communication from person to person and place to place can be difficult, and poor communication often leads to misunderstandings between people and regions.

Hindi is spoken by about 40 percent of the population, and English serves as the language of business. These 2 languages are the most important in India, but 14 other tongues also are mentioned in the constitution. Many of these are regional languages spoken primarily in one or two states, such as Bengali (Bengal), Punjabi (Punjab), and Kashmiri (Jammu and Kashmir). Twenty-four languages have over one million speakers, but others have only a handful of speakers and are in danger of being lost as the older people die.

Hindi alone has at least 13 different dialects. These can be so different that other Hindi speakers may not understand them. Think of having a Nigerian, American, Australian, Indian, Jamaican, and an Irish person all speaking English in the same room. Even though they are speaking the same language, the dialects are very different, making it difficult or impossible to understand everyone.

THE ROLE OF WOMEN

Women traditionally have held secondary status in India. Boys are preferred over girls in rural areas where it is widely believed that the more boys a family has, the better off they are. Much of a woman's identity traditionally has been tied to males in her family, particularly her husband. In the past, women often felt such a loss with the death of a husband that they would commit suicide by throwing themselves onto his funeral pyre. This practice, called *sati*, is outlawed in India today.

How did India choose a woman, Indira Gandhi, as prime minister? Her achievement is particularly remarkable when one considers that even many Western countries, such as the United States, have not yet elected a woman as head of state. Indira Gandhi was a remarkably bright leader who possessed all the

Most marriages are arranged by the two families involved, and the bride and groom frequently remain strangers until their wedding day. The wedding is seen as a contract between families, as each seeks to reinforce its status in India's class, or caste, system.

skills and knowledge necessary to serve as prime minister. However, most people believe that she never would have been selected had she not been the daughter of Jawaharlal Nehru, the first prime minister of India. No Indian woman has served, or has been proposed to serve, as the prime minister other than those connected to Nehru's family.

Life is difficult for the hardworking women in India's rural areas. They live under very rough conditions, hauling heavy containers of water by hand or on their heads, cooking, raising children, and tending to the daily needs of the family. Women receive significantly less education than males, and their choices are very limited. Urban women have more opportunities; the work environment is more accepting and many more women are well-educated.

Parents arrange most marriages in India. These marriages are more like a social contract, rather than a marriage based upon love and personal choice. The person who one marries may be a stranger. After the marriage, a rural woman usually moves to the husband's village and does menial work, receiving very low, if any, wages. Spousal abuse is common. Some women in higher castes are educated with the aim of getting a good husband. After marriage, they are expected to be the home-maker and mother above all else. Many double standards exist in the lives of men and women. If a woman divorces a man, she becomes a virtual outcast. No such fate befalls a man even he is cruel or causes the marriage to break up.

Another tragic and illegal practice has been dowry murders and suicides. When women marry, they traditionally go to live with the husband's family. At the time of the marriage, the woman's family presents a dowry, which is an array of gifts, such as cattle or other wealth, to the new husband for taking the woman as his wife. Dowry murders and suicides result when a husband's family harasses or even kills the wife and then keeps the dowry. The man then gets another wife and another dowry employing this horrible practice as a means to accumulate wealth. Sadly, police believe that over 6,000 dowry murders still take place in India each year.

Women of India adorn themselves in a variety of ways. One way that is somewhat unique to India is that of the *tika*, the marking or dot found on the forehead of many Hindu and Christian women. Married women wear the round small circle called a *bindi*. Even some men in India wear the tika. This marking can be put on with makeup. It also can be purchased in stores selling colorful and sometimes even exotic tikas that simply stick to a woman's forehead. The practice of wearing a tika has even been borrowed and popularized by Western entertainers looking to make themselves appear more exotic.

While life for women in India can be very grim, there are some signs of improvement. Women were first allowed to join the military in 1993, and today their roles in business are increas-ing. The number of women in parliament has been increasing steadily. At the same time, women exercise tremendous influence in their homes and there they have the opportunity to help their children develop values that will foster equality for women. But the path to equality for women is very long and much more work needs to be done by and for women in India.

ENTERTAINMENT

India has a rich cultural tradition of entertainment, including song and dance and the world's largest motion picture industry. Musically, stringed instruments like the sitar are traditional, but have been used by groups like the Beatles to add a mystical sound to Western music. Dance movements are very precise, with each movement of hands and feet carrying meaning. While music from the West can be heard in India, there is a huge and prosperous domestic music industry. There is even an Indian MTV station that broadcasts videos of Indian musicians and singers. The most popular modern songs tend to come from India's prolific movie industry.

Traditional music is often regional and may have social, religious, festive, or other uses. Two types of classical music are the most popular. One is music from northern India and called Hindustani, and the second is from the south and called Carnatic.

Dance is often tied to holidays and celebrations. Dancers dressed in rich costumes move gracefully with precise expressions and hand movements conveying traditional classical dances. Many different forms of dance exist in India, but each offers intriguing looks at the beauty and grace of the culture.

India is the world's greatest producer of films. Hundreds of films are produced each year with most coming out of "Bollywood," the name for India's movie-making industry in Mumbai. There are thousands of theaters across India with nearly every village having a cinema. Actors and actresses are nationally known and recognized and their lives are closely covered in magazines and on Internet web sites. Going to the movies is a very popular activity. India also exports its films to

India's thriving cultural life includes a rich tradition of music and dance. In Indian dance, each movement of the hands, feet, and body confers a special meaning.

other Asian nations, as well as to many countries where Indian citizens have emigrated. Some are also occasionally shown in the West.

Movies often are based on long love stories that have songs interwoven into the story. Romance, comedy, and violence are usually key ingredients. The movies usually are dramatic and long—often running for three hours. All of this allows people to escape from the rigors of daily life in India.

FOOD IN INDIA

Most Indians are vegetarians and few dishes contain meat. However, not all Hindus abstain from meat. Local breads, such as *chapati*, and vegetables with rice are diet mainstays for most

Indians. Chapati is flat bread that is eaten daily by most Indians. Wonderful spices like curry, chili, saffron, peppers, cloves, and coriander are used to flavor foods. Basic dietary staples such as vegetables or meats are usually products that are produced locally. Although fish is popular along the coasts, it is rare in diets elsewhere. Since refrigeration is not available to many Indians, fresh foods are bought daily in the market. Markets provide not only fresh foods, but also serve as a social gathering place for people. When traveling in India, most visitors find that the food seems to get spicier and hotter the farther south one goes.

Here is a recipe for Indian flat bread, or chapati:

2 cups whole wheat flour

1 cup warm water

pinch of salt

Put the flour and a pinch of salt in a large mixing bowl and add ½ cup of the warm water. Mix the two together and add the rest of the water until the mixture forms a ball. Knead the mix until it is smooth. Set the covered dough aside in a warm place for 30 minutes. Divide the dough into 10–12 equal parts and roll each ball into a flat piece of dough about 6 inches in diameter. The dough will look somewhat like flour tortillas. Using a very hot ungreased frying pan, cook each chapati piece for about 1 minute on the first side. When bubbles appear on the first side, the chapati should be turned over and cooked for about 45 seconds. The chapati is done when brown spots appear, or the dough begins to puff up in the pan. This recipe serves 6-8 people and is great to serve with curry, spiced foods, or other Asian dishes.

India's road to self-rule has not been an easy one. Early strife split Hindu and Muslim factions into separate areas, with many Muslims fleeing to what is now Pakistan. The parliamentary system that survives today bears many similarities to the governing bodies of both England and the United States.

6

Government

James Madison, the second American president, once said, "If men were angels, there would be no need for government." Understanding this quote makes it easier to make sense of India's government, or any other. India was born amidst chaos in August 1947. Instead of an independence celebration for the ages, tragedy took place. Before independence, Lord Louis Mountbatten, the last British viceroy in India, had divided India into two regions, one for Muslims and one for Hindus. The provinces of Bengal in the east and Punjab in the west were split. This fueled a conflict over land claims and started the largest migration in recent human history, with more than 17 million people taking flight. Muslims fled Hindu India, moving to those provinces that soon would become Pakistan. The migration of Hindus was in the opposite direction as they moved to places that would remain a part of Hindu-dominated India. India was also struggling to restore calm after violence between Muslims and Hindus. Soon after there was fighting with the new country of Pakistan over rival land claims to Kashmir and Jammu. Tragically, the great Indian peacemaker, Mohandas K. Gandhi, was assassinated in January 1948. With his tragic death, one of the world's great moral and spiritual leaders no longer served as a bridge to peace between the two antagonistic religious factions. Independence was a time of short-lived joy.

When the British left after more than 250 years of colonial rule, India needed to become self-governing. A new constitution was written by 1949 and adopted by the emerging nation in 1950. The constitution was patterned largely after that of the United States, but it also preserved many elements from the British and included many special features uniquely suited to India.

FEDERAL GOVERNMENT

The constitution established India's government as a federal republic. A federal system divides the powers between the national government and smaller governmental units such as states and local governments. A republic is a political system in which the voters hold power, but elected representatives do the actual work of governing. These elected individuals are responsible for promoting the well-being of society. Thus, India is a representative democracy that divides the powers of government between the central and local governments.

Parliament and the Prime Minister

India's parliamentary form of government is similar to that of the British. There are two houses of parliament, creating a bicameral system. The lower house is called the Lok Sabha

(House of the People) and the upper house is called the Rajya Sabha (Council of States). The Lok Sabha has 550 members (including the Speaker of the House), and the Rajya Sabha has 250 members.

Members of the Rajya Sabha are democratically elected for six-year terms with one-third of the members being elected every two years, primarily by the state legislatures. The constitution also allows the president to appoint 12 members of the Rajya Sabha. These members are chosen as experts with special knowledge in fields such as science, literature, or the social services. Members of the Rajya Sabha must be at least 30 years old.

Members of the Lok Sabha must be at least 25 years old and are elected directly by the voters for five-year terms. All Indians over the age of 18 have the right to vote. The territories elect 20 members of the Lok Sabha, while the other 530 members are elected from India's 25 states. The prime minister and members of the cabinet are chosen from the membership of the parliament. The prime minister serves at the pleasure of the parliament and is responsible to it.

India also has a president, but this office holds very little power. The constitution provides the president with some authority, primarily in emergency situations. Most of the president's job is ceremonial. The prime minister and his cabinet lead India's executive branch of government on a day-to-day basis. Historically, the prime minister frequently has come from the family of Jawaharlal Nehru. The Nehru family's popularity and its long hold on the prime minister's position are sometimes referred to as the House of Nehru. Even though India is the world's largest democracy, the Nehru family has controlled the prime minister's position for most of the country's history. Some say that they have become India's version of a royal family. In the years since the assassination of Indira Gandhi's son, Rajiv, while he was campaigning for reelection in 1991, many have encouraged his widow, Sonia, to become prime minister. A native of Italy, she has continued to play an important role in the political leadership in India.

The Role of Parliament

The Lok Sabha must meet at least twice a year according to the constitution, with no more than six months between meetings. The Lok Sabha is unique in that it is the only house that can initiate financial legislation. Other than that, the powers of the two houses are not much different. The constitution lists a number of powers for parliament, and both houses are responsible. Some specific powers of the parliament include:

- The ability to meet together in a joint sitting and vote together. This action has the same effect as if both houses had passed a bill separately. A bill is a proposed law that is being considered by a legislative body. After bills are passed by the Parliament, they become law after the president signs them.

- The ability to fix or change state boundaries.

- The responsibility for amending or changing the constitution, as needed.

- The removal of the cabinet and prime minister, if necessary, by a vote of no confidence.

- The responsibility to make laws for India in accordance with the powers provided in the constitution.

Judicial Branch

The judicial branch of government is responsible for interpreting a country's laws. In India, as in the United States, the highest court is the Supreme Court. This court is composed of a chief justice and up to seven other justices. Unlike in the United States, India's parliament can increase the number of justices by changing the law. The president appoints the justices

The two houses of India's parliament are much like the U.S. Congress, one representing the people, one the states. Unlike the United States, however, the office of president in India holds little power and is largely ceremonial.

of the Supreme Court. Usually this is done after the president discusses the selection with the judges on the Supreme Court and judges in the high courts of the states. The prime minister and others often apply political pressure on the selections, so the process can become very complicated. Supreme Court judges may serve until age 65. Judges also may be removed from office if they are found guilty of misbehavior, or if they are unable to serve because of health reasons.

The Supreme Court has two sources of cases. The first is original jurisdiction. This means that the Supreme Court can hear some cases when they are presented for the first time in a courtroom. Situations in which the Indian Supreme Court has original jurisdiction include:

- Disputes that arise between the national government and one or more states.

- Disputes where the national government and one or more state governments are in a dispute with another state or states.

- Disputes between two or more states.

The Supreme Court also has appellate jurisdiction. This term refers to court cases that have been heard by lower courts, but the decision, or verdict, has been appealed to the Supreme Court. Most cases that the Supreme Court hears come by the appeals process. The Supreme Court can decide whether to accept or reject cases that are appealed from other courts. They will accept cases that address important aspects of law, or constitutional issues in an effort to bring finality to vital legal questions. When they refuse to take an appeal, it means that they support the lower court ruling.

The president of India may also ask the Supreme Court for advice on important national issues that involve a question of law. The court then can provide a legal opinion to the president on the matter.

STATE AND LOCAL GOVERNMENTS

India has 25 states. Each state has a governmental structure similar to that of the national government. Each has a state constitution that establishes the legislative, executive, and judicial branches. Some of the states have bicameral legislatures with two houses. Others have unicameral legislatures with only one house. Members of these legislative assemblies are elected directly by the citizens in their district. The terms of office can extend to five years, unless the government is dissolved earlier.

The legislative bodies, like the national parliament, create the laws for their state. Bills become laws when passed by the state legislative bodies and when the state's governor signs them into law.

The president appoints governors to five-year terms. Their primary role is to serve as a representative of the national government. Governors hold limited power and the office is largely ceremonial. Most executive power is held by the state's council of ministers, which serves much like the cabinet at the national level. Each state has a chief minister who serves as the primary leader of the executive branch. Their executive role at the state level is similar to the prime minister's at the national level.

Within the 25 states there is another governmental subdivision called the district; there are 476 districts in India. Districts vary in size and population, but they average having over two million people. Most districts have between 200 and 600 villages within their territory. The district collector is the most powerful local district official. He maintains law and order, coordinates district departments, and collects taxes. District and other local governing bodies are under the authority of the state government that delegates responsibilities to local officials.

Local governments are not all organized and governed in the same way throughout India. Some have governing bodies called boards, committees, or even corporations. Village councils called *panchayats* have been developed in recent years in an effort to pass more resources directly to local governments. This has been developed to help improve life in rural areas where nearly 75 percent of the country's population lives. This system gives more power to rural communities to solve local problems, such as creating jobs and increasing citizen participation. Panchayat members are elected for five-year terms.

Cities are home to only about 25 percent of India's population. Municipal corporations and municipal councils are composed of elected officials who govern the cities. Each municipal corporation or council also elects a president or a mayor from its membership to head the body.

POLITICAL PARTIES

India has a multiparty political system. Unlike the United States, where there are two dominant political parties, India has many parties, each of which has its own perspective on how government should be run. These parties come in all colors, shapes, and sizes, which reflects the great diversity found within India's population. The House of Nehru has been the Congress Party. Historically it has been India's strongest political party. Surprisingly, the Congress Party has never received a majority of the votes or seats in parliament. They have always needed to build a coalition with other parties. This means that they agree to form a partnership, with one or more other political parties, which allows them to form a government and rule India. The most successful opposition parties to the Congress Party have, in reality, been opposition coalitions of two or more political parties. All of this is very different from the United States, where either of the two parties is elected with a majority and runs the government. No coalition of political parties is necessary in the United States, but it is a political reality in India.

A political group that has been increasing in strength is the Bharatiya Janata Party (BJP). This is the leading Hindu nationalist party. When relations with Pakistan become tense, the Bharatiya Janata Party tends to gain strength. This causes Muslims and moderate Hindus in India to become fearful, as they believe the party is a threat to the interests of a multi-religious India. The prime minister's position has been held by a BJP member at times in the late 1990s. In 1998, during the rule of the Bharatiya Janata Party and their nationalist prime minister, Atal Bihari Vajpayee, India conducted five nuclear weapon tests. This brought worldwide condemnation and frightened Pakistan into also conducting nuclear bomb tests only two weeks later. A year later both governments tested missiles capable of carrying nuclear bombs. Thus, the rise of the Bharatiya Janata Party has increased tensions even further on the Indian subcontinent.

The roots of the BJP go back to 1925 to a nationalist organization called the Rashtriya Swayamsevak Sangh (RSS), which means National Volunteer Organization. The RSS was very critical of Mohandas K. Gandhi's leadership, which advocated nonviolence and civil disobedience to impel the British to leave. Tragically, it was one of the RSS party members who assassinated Mohandas Gandhi. The party was then banned for over a year. The Bharatiya Janata Party today is the modern voice of the nationalist cause originally championed by the RSS.

The Communist Party of India has been active since 1925. The party traditionally has been strong in the states of West Bengal and Kerala. At times the Communist Party has led the governments in these two states, sometimes in coalition with other leftist parties. The Communist Party has lost strength nationally in recent years, but it continues to operate within India's democratic system with some success in southern India. Other political parties in India have a national base, but receive a very low percentage of votes. Many of these smaller parties have specific issues that they promote, or ties that limit their broad appeal.

The Congress Party is well positioned within India's political spectrum. With the BJP party on the political right and the Communist Party on the political left, the Congress Party holds the moderate center in Indian politics. Coalitions are necessary to form governments and it is easier to form them at the middle of the political range. This factor also tends to keep the power of the parties and government in balance. As in all true democracies, citizens shape the future when they cast their votes.

Rights and Responsibilities of Citizens

The fundamental rights of the citizen are protected in India much as they are in the United States. These rights are held above any other law of the land and include:

- Equality before the law.
- Freedom of speech.
- Freedom of association and peaceful assembly.
- Freedom of religion.
- Freedom of movement within the country.
- The right to live in India where a citizen chooses and select the occupation he or she desires.
- Protection from discrimination on the basis of religion, caste, sex, race, or place of birth.
- The right not to be a witness against himself/herself.
- The abolishment of untouchability.
- The prohibition of forced labor or trafficking of people.

Freedom of speech also implies freedom of the press in India. In addition to the above freedoms, other rights are given to minorities to protect aspects of their culture, such as their language and their ability to have their own educational systems. All of these freedoms have limitations. This prevents citizens from being harmed by other persons who try to push their own rights too far. This is similar to the United States where freedom of speech does not allow a citizen to tell lies about or slander another person. Such acts are considered beyond the protection of free speech. The people of India also once had the right to property, but this right was changed in 1978 by an amendment, which stated, "No person shall be deprived of his property, save [but] by authority of law."

In all societies, rights do not come to citizens without responsibilities. In India, the constitution also provides for the following responsibilities for citizens in the list of fundamental duties:

- To abide by the constitution and respect its ideals and institutions, the national flag, and the national anthem.

- To cherish and follow the noble ideals that inspired our national struggle for freedom.

- To uphold and protect the sovereignty, unity, and integrity of India.

- To defend the country and render national service when called upon to do so.

- To promote harmony and the spirit of common brotherhood amongst all the people of India transcending religious, linguistic, and regional or sectional diversities; to renounce practices derogatory to the dignity of women.

- To value and preserve the rich heritage of our composite culture.

- To protect and improve the natural environment including forests, lakes, rivers and wildlife, and to have compassion for living creatures.

- To develop the scientific temper, humanism, and the spirit of inquiry and reform.

- To safeguard public property and to abjure (renounce) violence;

- To strive toward excellence in all spheres of individual and collective activity so that the nation constantly rises to higher levels of endeavor and achievement.

The United States and many other nations do not include a listing of the fundamental duties of all citizens in their constitutions. Do you believe this is important to include?

FOREIGN AFFAIRS

India is a key nation in the world today because of its population, power, and importance in international affairs. It is a member of the United Nations and has often served on the powerful Security Council. In addition, it has participated actively in United Nations peacekeeping forces in areas such as the Middle East, Congo, and Cyprus.

India's most important relationship in the 1940s and 1950s was with its former colonial master, the United Kingdom. Prime Minister Nehru was wary, however, of being too dependent upon the United Kingdom when the long years of colonial rule ended in 1947. In the mid-1950s, under the leadership of Prime Minister Nehru, India began a movement that was composed of many colonies and newly independent countries that worked against taking sides during the Cold War, a period that lasted from 1945 until 1991. This non-alignment movement was formally established in 1961. The Cold War era saw the United States and the Soviet Union pitted against each other in many locations around the world. India remained a leader in this movement until the Cold War ended with the disintegration of the Soviet Union in 1991. With this breakup, the original purpose for the non-aligned movement ceased to exist. The movement has tried to focus on other issues in recent years, but it has become less influential in the post-Soviet era.

Poised at the west and northeast of India are two very powerful nuclear neighbors, Pakistan and China. India's past relationships with these two powers have been filled with conflict and strained relations. The relationships between India, Pakistan, and China were a part of the larger Cold War conflict. During the Cold War, Pakistan allied with the

India's relationship to the neighboring countries of Pakistan and China has often been strained. In 2001, Pakistan and India stood on the brink of armed conflict, but were able to manage their differences peacefully. Meeting in 2001 for a summit to discuss their differences, Pakistani President Musharraf (left) is greeted by Indian Prime Minister Vajpayee.

United States, while India, which was theoretically non-aligned, stayed closer to the Soviet Union. The Soviet Union, in turn, was often at odds with China. This presented a terrifying prospect at the time, as five of the most powerful nations vied with one another around the world for power and influence.

When the Cold War ended in 1991, the conflict with Pakistan over Kashmir continued. India accused Pakistan of aiding rebels in this northern region and acts of terrorism frequently still take place in this area. India and Pakistan have even fought over possession of the Siachen Glacier. Talks are often held between India and Pakistan on the future of Kashmir and other long-standing disputes, but progress is rare and tensions remain high today. This presents both countries, as well as the world, with the frightening prospect of two nuclear powers being on the verge of war.

Relations between India and China have been calmer in recent years, but can heat up very quickly. After independence, India tried to establish a close relationship with China, but this fell apart when China asserted territorial claims over Tibet, an area that served as a buffer between the two giant nations. War broke out when China attacked India in October 1962. During this war, China moved far into India's northeast, coming within 30 miles of the Assam plains and other strategic areas. In 1965, China supported Pakistan in its war with India. Relations between the India and China continued to be strained until the 1980s, when China aligned itself more closely with Pakistan, whereas India linked itself with the Soviet Union, which then posed a threat to China.

Then Prime Minister Rajiv Gandhi traveled to China in late 1988 and initiated new talks between the nations. Relations between India and China slowly improved during the 1990s, with communication and travel becoming more frequent between the countries. Serious attempts to resolve the border issues in the northeast have continued with both sides express-ing optimism.

India also is a member of the South Asian Association for Regional Cooperation (SAARC). This group consists of India, Pakistan, Bangladesh, Nepal, Bhutan, Sri Lanka, and the Maldives. The group does not deal with two-party conflicts, such as that existing between Pakistan and India. It focuses on broad issues like transportation, science and technology, agriculture, culture and sport, abuse, drug trafficking, telecommunications, and terrorism. This group's effectiveness has been hampered because a unanimous vote is required before action can be taken. The inability to address conflicts between member nations also limits the association's effectiveness.

India struggles today with many issues of conflict, discrimination, intolerance, and violence. The need for good government is obvious in India. With over a billion people, India has great economic challenges. India's people and its government are working to promote a healthy economy.

Providing sufficient food, shelter, and products for a population of over one billion remains a challenge for India. Farming is the most stable income source in India's economy, providing a livelihood for two-thirds of the people.

7

India's Economy

Providing food, clothing, and shelter for a billion citizens would be a staggering task for any country. Although India can produce enough food to feed itself, poverty is widespread. From the slums of Mumbai (Bombay) to the people sleeping on the streets of Calcutta, poverty is an everyday social and economic reality in India. Yet, both the richest of the rich and the poorest of the poor call India home.

ECONOMIC OVERVIEW

Many things have changed in India's economy since independence, but one element that has remained stable is agriculture. Two-thirds of India's people are engaged in farming. Farms are very small by American standards; many, in fact, would hardly be called farms in the United States as they resemble home gardens.

The most important change in the economy has been the transition from a centrally controlled system to one that is more of a free market. Centrally controlled economies have most of the economic planning done by the government. The government may own factories, transportation and communication systems, mines, and other key elements of the economy. They can even set prices for goods, products, and services.

Today, India has moved to a mixed economy, with greater ownership of property by the private sector. Economic decisions and prices are controlled to a greater degree by supply and demand than they are by government policy. This type of economic system makes India much more competitive in the global marketplace, as prices of goods and services more truly reflect the costs of production.

A large well-educated population can be a great asset to a country's economy. India has made great strides in recent years with the advent of telecommuting. Today, a doctor in Los Angeles may write up his daily notes and send them electronically to a doctor in India who reviews the notes and offers opinions on the case while the doctor is sleeping in California. The Indian doctor sends his review to the American doctor who uses the information to treat his patient the next day. Labor is much cheaper in India than in many other countries. This allows creative and talented Indian workers to work on-line and send their work to their employer in the United States, Europe, or elsewhere.

AGRICULTURE

At the time of independence, agriculture was the most important part of India's economy. More than 70 percent of the population was involved in agriculture in the mid-1900s. Millions of poor people worked on small plots of land. Some owned their own land, but most worked on land belonging to others. Even with so many people engaged in farming, India was unable to feed its people. Foreign aid was required to supplement the farming production and to feed the population. Famine was commonplace and widespread. Farmers grew millet, rice, wheat, barley, corn, sugar cane, cotton, jute (fiber used to make sacks or twine), and other crops.

Agriculture is still king in India's economy today. However, many changes have taken place. India now can farm over 50 percent of its land, and over half of the population is still engaged in agriculture. Unfortunately, agriculture only generates about 20 percent of India's gross domestic product (GDP) today. Much of the farming is still done by hand with very little modern machinery being used to plant or harvest crops. Since the arrival of the green revolution during the 1960s and 1970s, however, production has steadily improved. Farming advances include increased irrigation, and the use of improved fertilizers, pesticides, and high-yield seeds. Rice, wheat, cotton, sugar and many of the traditional products are still grown. India is also a major exporter of spices, tea, and coffee. With the changes and improvements that have taken place, India now produces enough grain to feed its people. This is a truly remarkable turn of events in a country where the population has tripled during the past half-century.

Forestry, fishing, and dairy farming are also important to India's economy. Water buffalo, cattle, goats, and sheep are raised and are frequently seen roaming the streets of even India's largest cities. Most of these animals are not raised for eating, as this is forbidden for Hindus. However, their milk is consumed and some of the animals are used for labor, such as pulling plows in the fields. Animal manure is also dried and ued as fuel.

MANUFACTURING

Today, India has a very diversified manufacturing sector. Wages are low by international standards and this allows the country to produce manufactured goods at very reasonable export prices. Items produced include textiles, cement, steel, vehicles, ships, fertilizers, appliances, and chemicals. Clothing and other textiles make up about 25 percent of the exports, while electronics and computer software are becoming increasingly important. Private owners now hold most of the companies that produce manufacturing and consumer products.

India's high-tech industries manufacture such things as space satellites and nuclear power plants. Most of these high-tech and strategic businesses are under the control of the government, a holdover from earlier times when the economy was more centrally controlled.

Pollution is a big problem for many of India's industries. Polluted air, water, and soil are caused by older factories and by the smoke produced by people simply cooking their meals over open fires. Considering that there are hundreds of millions of poor Indians who have no choice other than to cook their food and purify water over open fires, this is a huge problem.

NATURAL RESOURCES

Manufacturing industries feed on natural resources. They consume everything from the energy needed to power a factory's machines to the steel needed to make the machines. Many different minerals are extracted in India. India is among the world's leaders in the mining of iron and coal. In addition to iron ore, the metals produced include copper, manganese, bauxite, titanium, chromium, lead, and zinc. There also are deposits of diamonds and other gemstones. Unfortunately, there is a shortage of petroleum. Some production of petroleum and natural gas along with coal provides essential energy supplies, but there is not enough to meet the country's needs.

TOURISM

Travel in India can be quite challenging for tourists. Visitors must be patient as transportation can have long delays and hotels may be both expensive and not up to the

Modern industry demands fuel, such as that provided by this natural gas plant. Yet India's energy needs exceed the supply, and a shortage of petroleum continues to challenge the nation to discover new energy sources.

level expected by visitors in some classes of accommodation. However, the rewards for visitors are unparalleled. From the rugged snow-capped Himalayas in the north and beautiful Dal Lake at their base, to the sand beaches that stretch across India's south, the country is blessed with a cornucopia of treasures for tourists.

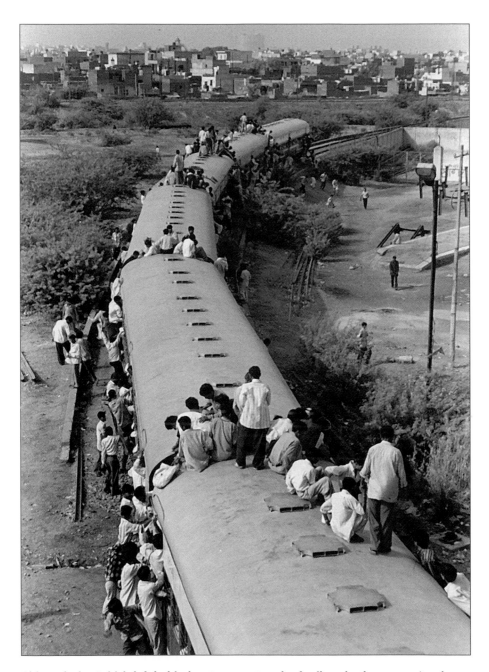

Although the British left behind a strong network of railroads, the gauge (track width) of these systems is not standardized, forcing passengers and freight to switch from one train to another on longer trips. Overcrowding frequently results in scenes like this one, where passengers are forced to ride outside the train.

and carbon into an already polluted atmosphere. Some people drive scooters, mopeds, and motorcycles, which are cheaper two-wheeled vehicles. There are also three-wheeled cycle-rickshaws that have motorcycle fronts and two-passenger backseats with two wheels. The "tempos" are larger, with as many as six or more seats in the back and they usually serve regular routes. Most of the three-wheeled vehicles are more dangerous than cars as they are prone to tip over on fast corners. Buses are also used to travel within and between cities.

Air travel is available within India and for international travel. Since India is a large country, air travel is a much faster means of getting between cities. But the cost of flying is beyond the reach of most Indians. India Airlines is the country's only international carrier. Other countries' international carriers provide some competition as direct flights come in to Mumbai and Delhi from Paris, London, Rome, Frankfurt, Hong Kong, Singapore, and many other cities. Direct flights from North America are rare because of the tremendous distance. Most people traveling from North America will make connecting flights in Europe or Asia that go on to India.

COMMUNICATION

Communication systems provide a foundation for economic systems as businesses, factories, and consumers all are connected by the systems operating within a country. In India, the traditional systems like telephone, mail, fax, and e-mail are available, but not all citizens can afford them. Cell phones are becoming increasingly popular because they do not need the cable and wire links required by traditional telephone systems. Many evolving economies have been able to skip a generation of telephone technology by going directly to cell phones.

Mass communication is provided by newspapers, magazines, television, and radio. Newspapers exist in many different languages and even people in the United States can read English versions of Indian newspapers via the Internet. Using the following Internet addresses, one can take a virtual trip to India:

The Times of India (New Delhi)   www.timesofindia.com

Hindustan Times (New Delhi)   www.hindustantimes.com

The Telegraph (Calcutta)   www.telegraphindia.com

The Indian Express (Mumbai)   www.indianexpress.com

Greater Kashmir (Srinagar)   www.greaterkashmir.com

National television and radio broadcasting were formerly controlled by the central government. During this time, politicians often abused the media by using it for their own political purposes. This problem has helped to increase the flow of information now available from other television stations that are broadcast from satellites. Starting in the early 1990s, India gained access to programming that includes the international version of CNN, an Indian version of MTV, and other programming from Western nations.

TRADE

India has many trading partners including both the United States and Russia. The European Union and Japan have recently become important trading partners. The United States, however, leads in trade with India, accounting for about one-sixth of all exports and imports.

Much of India's trade comes via the major seaports in India. Large containers are loaded with goods and then shipped to ports around the world where they are unloaded and carried away by rail or trucks.

The primary exports include clothing, gems, agricultural products, leather products, iron ore, and other minerals. India also imports many things including petroleum from the Middle East, and such things as chemicals, fertilizers, and paper products from countries around the world.

One of India's major exports is its talented work force. Unable to find good jobs that pay well at home, many Indian engineers, doctors, and scientists emigrate to Western countries in search of better opportunities. Unfortunately, this means that India loses many of its most educated and talented citizens.

India's stock market has become more active in recent years as private ownership has increased. Individuals within India and overseas can now buy shares of stock in Indian companies that they believe will turn a profit.

India would appear to have many strikes against it in terms of achieving a state of economic well-being in the near future. More than one billion people are tightly packed into an area the size of the United States east of the Mississippi River. This severely limits available space for personal use, agricultural development, and room to expand. A rapidly growing population in search of land, water, and other resources needed to survive has pushed much of the natural environment to the breaking point. Petroleum resources essential for economic growth are limited. Transportation and communication linkages, although adequate, remain quite inefficient. Yet, in spite of this, India's economy has exploded since the country gained its independence during the mid-twentieth century. Today, most of India's people are much better off than were most Indians a half-century ago. Both the country and its people are quite optimistic about their economic future.

Although most of India's population is rural, there are many thriving cities. Indian cities, such as Delhi, are huge commercial, political, and religious centers, providing some relief from the poverty and low literacy rates found in rural areas.

Cities in India

I t is hard to imagine that with a population of over a billion people India is still primarily rural. Most of India's people still live outside of the cities. In these rural areas, poverty is a problem and few people can read and write. Literacy for the entire nation is barely over 50 percent, although it is much higher in cities. The average income is a meager $1,600 per year or only about $125 a month. Income for city workers can be considerably higher.

India's people shape and use their land in a variety of ways. Over half of the land is available for farming and nearly two-thirds of the population is engaged in agriculture. The human imprint, or cultural landscape, is very obvious throughout nearly

The former British capital in India is Calcutta, whose brief history has included bouts with severe poverty, pollution, and overcrowding. Nonetheless, the city has a thriving creative community and is home to many writers, artists, and filmmakers who draw on the city as a source for their creative energy.

The people of this city often make it an inspirational place that teaches others the best of humanity.

With the challenging cultural environment in Calcutta, it is perhaps surprising that the arts have done well here. Many writers, artists, philosophers and filmmakers produce their creative works in Calcutta as the city serves as a source of creative energy. While Mumbai is like the hands of a person, producing and doing, Calcutta views itself more like the mind—thinking and creating.

DELHI

Delhi, India's third-largest city, is the country's capital and political heart. The city offers a spectacular mosaic of buildings, temples, and memorials that reveal many fascinating chapters in India's history. Delhi has served as a center of political power at various times over a span of 3,000 years. This long history has left many interesting sites scattered throughout the city. Among the better-known historical sites are: the Red Fort, Indira Gandhi Memorial Museum, Parliament House, the Raj Ghat (the place where Mohandas Gandhi was assassinated), and one of Asoka's pillars. For a few rupees (one rupee is worth $0.02 in U.S. currency), a visitor can catch a cab or other local transportation and fill the day with interesting places to see and history to explore.

The city is divided into Old Delhi and New Delhi. The older part of the city has a rich and deep history that provides the character of the city's past. New Delhi has the capital and is more modern in aspect. People with political power walk the streets, deals are made, and big business is conducted in New Delhi's houses of government and commerce.

Delhi is also a major transportation hub for the country. Over 30 international airlines fly in and out of Indira Gandhi International Airport on the city's edge. Domestic airlines also use Delhi as their hub, as do most other forms of transportation including rail, buses, and the road system.

Delhi also faces the issues of poverty and of ever more people moving into the city. Like most Indian cities, the contrasts between the richest of the rich and the poorest of the poor are great.

VARANASI (BENARES)

Some people believe that Varanasi is the world's oldest continuously inhabited city. It is also India's most holy city and a world religious center for Hindus. Varanasi rests on the banks of the Ganges River where Hindus make their pilgrimage to bathe in the river's waters throughout the year. It is believed that bathing in the river cleanses one of sin.

Early in the morning, thousands of people climb down the steep steps of the Ghats that line the Ganges in Varanasi. Women in saris and men in loincloths enter the water to bathe and wash away all of the sins of their lifetime. They seem to be unaware of the many noises and scenes around them as they focus intently upon their cleansing. A short distance away the dead are cremated and the ashes are collected and released into the Ganges. Dying here is considered a fortunate event to Hindus, because of the belief that the deceased will not be reincarnated, but instead will go directly to heaven. A dead cow, considered holy, floats down the river with beautiful flowers strewn about its body. This scene can be disturbing to visitors, but the Hindus seem oblivious to worldly concerns. They will brush their teeth and drink from the water just a few steps away from these other activities. A visit to Varanasi is an unforgettable experience.

OTHER CITIES

There are a number of other great cities and places in India including Srinagar in the north. Situated on Dal Lake, the city has a beautiful view of the towering Himalayas in the distance. The northern city of Agra has the Taj Mahal, while Trivandrum is near the southernmost point in India and is known for its beautiful beaches. Madras, India's fourth-largest city, has one of the world's largest rock relief sculptures located only 28 miles away in Mamallapuram. Only Mt. Rushmore in the United

States is larger. St. Thomas died near Madras. Legend holds that he died from a spear that struck him while he was praying before a cross on St. Thomas Mount.

India has many fascinating and busy places. The incongruity of grinding poverty and great wealth is evident throughout the country, but the wealth of India's fascinating history and varied cultures is overwhelming.

While India's future remains uncertain, the mood expressed by these children offers hope. Dressed in the traditional attire of Hindus, Muslims, and Sikhs, they celebrate the unity and diversity of India's cultural groups.

India
Looks Ahead

Predicting the future of any country is a precarious and inexact science. This is especially true in the case of India. There are a number of possible future scenarios for the country. Some may be quite optimistic, while others are very pessimistic in terms of possible outcomes. An already huge population that doubles every 40 years creates a staggering challenge for the future. Conflict resulting from religious and other cultural differences creates its own set of challenges. Any glimpse of the future must consider the dangers posed by the presence of India's neighbors, Pakistan and China, poised on its borders with nuclear military capability.

Population problems alone will require talent and creativity on the part of India's democratic government to solve. The prospect of a population exceeding two billion people by 2050 is a distinct reality for India. At the current rate of growth, the country's population will surpass that of China in about two decades. India has been able to feed its people through the end of the twentieth century. Whether it will be able to continue to do so depends on many factors. Further innovations in food technology such as fertilizer, improved seeds, and other farming improvements may help with the task. At the same time, increasing urbanization is taking more and more land out of production. Huge areas around Mumbai and many other Indian cities are poverty stricken, as people leave rural areas in search of a better life in the city. In spite of this, an Indian's average life span has increased since independence in 1947 and can be expected to continue on this path.

India's educational system is key to helping create the jobs that will be needed in the twenty-first century. The promise of technology is realized now only by a small part of the population. The future may bring more jobs in technology to India if the country can provide a talented and well-educated labor force. Literacy remains a big problem, especially for women. Approximately half the population cannot read or write. A huge pool of semiskilled workers, however, is attractive to industries paying low wages. Low wages for even highly talented workers make India attractive to foreign investors. In addition, the increasing role of the free market in India with little governmental interference also can encourage industrial growth.

The amount of pollution generated by a billion people also spells trouble for India's future. The pollution creates additional health problems and decreases the average age of the population. Pollution of the land, air, and water is very evident throughout India, and it poses a huge threat to the well-being of society. Even the majestic Taj Mahal is threatened by pollution from nearby factories and traffic. The beautiful white marble is turning yellow and some of the inlaid stones are disappearing as the Taj Mahal deteriorates in a bath of corrosive smog. Recent efforts have attempted to create a protective zone around the monument, and they have met with some success. However, the difficult issues related to pollution affect not only the city of Agra and the Taj Mahal, but all of India's cities and many of the agricultural areas as well.

Political stability is another prerequisite for foreign investment in any nation. Before investors are willing to put money into a country's economy, they want to ensure that there are few risks. Having a democratic government that has survived more than a half-century of often turbulent times speaks well for India. The uncertainty created by the ongoing conflicts between India and Pakistan over Kashmir and other internal issues threaten the stability that investors love. In 2002 alone, over 60,000 Americans were encouraged to leave India because of the high risk of an impending war with Pakistan. If such a war should ever take place in the twenty-first century, it would present great peril not only to India and Pakistan, but to the entire world. Both countries now possess nuclear weapons and missiles capable of delivering warheads to each other's territory. If such a war should take place, the consequences would be devastating, with millions dying immediately and horrible long-term effects from nuclear contamination to the land and people.

A preferred future for India would be one in which

India and Pakistan come to the peace table and negotiate their differences. This process could resolve the long-standing land disputes over Kashmir. Instead of squandering the cost of millions of soldiers facing each other across a hostile border, money could be used to address such problems as poverty, pollution, and population growth. Relations with Pakistan serve as the biggest wild card in India's future.

The animosity between many Hindus and Muslims is now almost 1,000 years old. This conflict not only fuels the fire between India and Pakistan, but also presents India with domestic conflicts. A preferred future would have Indians becoming more tolerant of religious differences and also caste differences. Efforts to prevent and remedy religious and caste conflicts also consume economic resources that could be used more productively. The constitution provides for religious freedom and abolishes castes, but people still hold old customs and prejudices. Education can help to reduce these tensions by promoting cultural understanding and tolerance. These processes are slow and can be waylaid by people with hostile intentions.

Positive changes for women are also painfully slow in coming. A double standard is found throughout Indian society. Vast human resources are being wasted due to discrimination that does not place the same value on male and female achievement. With less education and opportunity, some of the most talented Indian people, who happen to be women, will not be able to help create a stronger country. Statistics show that when female literacy increases, birth rates drop sharply. This factor alone could help to slow the population growth and increase the quality of life in India.

Just as India presents a mystery to many outside

observers because of its vast diversity and complexity, so, too, the future remains shrouded in mystery. Choosing and creating the preferred future is a complex task. As the country's past has amply illustrated, unexpected events can bring about great and rapid change. India has great potential. Will that potential be realized? Only time will tell.

Facts at a Glance

Country Name	Republic of India
Location	Southern Asia, south of the Himalayas and facing the Arabian Sea and Bay of Bengal, and bordered, from west to east, by Pakistan, China, Nepal, Bangladesh, and Myanmar (Burma)
Capital	New Delhi
Area	1,229,737 square miles (3,287,590 square kilometers) Figures quoted in other sources may vary, because of contested territory.
Land Features	Himalayas and associated ranges; central and southern uplands, including Deccan Plateau; lowland plains of Indus, Ganges, and Brahmaputra rivers; Great Indian (Thar) Desert. Highest elevation: Mt. Kanchenjunga, 28,208 feet (8,598 meters)
Climate	Primarily tropical and subtropical, ranging from desert to humid; influenced primarily by monsoons, bringing moist summers and dry winters
Major Water Features	Ganges River, Punjab (headwaters of Indus River), Brahmaputra River; many reservoirs; glacial lakes in Himalayas
Natural Hazards	Floods, earthquakes, droughts, cyclones (hurricanes)
Land Use	Arable land: 57%
	Forest and woodland: 23%
	Permanent pastures: 4%
	Urban, waste, other: 16%
Environmental Issues	Deforestation, soil erosion, overgrazing, desertification, air and water pollution, overtaxing of natural resource base
Population	1,045,000,000 (July 2002 estimate)
Population Growth Rate	1.7% per year (approximately 17-18 million people per year)
Total Fertility Rate	3.04 (average number of children born to each woman during childbearing years)
Life Expectancy at Birth	63 years (male, 62; female 64)
Ethnic Groups	Indo-Aryan, 72%; Dravidian, 25%; other, 3%
Religion	Hindu, 81%; Muslim, 12%; Christian, 2%; Sikh, 2%; other groups including Buddhist, Jain, Parsi, 3%

Languages	English is the most important language for national, political, and business communication; Hindi is the national language and primary tongue of 30% of the people; other official languages include: Bengali, Telugu, Marathi, Tamil, Urdu, Gujarati, Malayalam, Kannada, Oriya, Punjabi, Assamese, Kashmiri, Sindhi, Sanskrit, Hindustani; several hundred lesser languages also are spoken
Literacy	Total population, 52%; male, 66%; female, 38%
Type of Government	Federal republic
Executive Branch	Chief of state: President (elected by both houses of parliament and state legislatures to 5-year term) Head of government: Prime Minister (elected by majority party members of parliament to 5-year term)
Independence	15 August 1947 (from the United Kingdom)
Administrative Divisions	28 states and 7 union territories
Currency	Indian rupee
Labor Force by Occupation	Agriculture: 67% Services: 18% Industry: 15%
Industries	Textiles, chemicals, food processing, steel, transportation equipment, cement, mining, petroleum, machinery, software
Primary Exports	Textiles, gems and jewelry, engineering goods, chemicals, leather goods
Export Partners	($43 billion, 2000 estimate) United States, 22%; UK, 6%; Japan, 5%; China, 5%
Imports	($61 billion, 2000 estimate) Crude oil, machinery, gems, fertilizer, chemicals
Import Partners	United States, 9%; Benelux (Belgium–Netherlands–Luxembourg), 8%; United Kingdom, 6%; Saudi Arabia, 6%; Japan, 6%; Germany 5%
Transportation	Highways (total): 2,062,730 miles (3,319,644 kilometers) Highway (paved): 942,668 miles (1,517,077 kilometers) Railroad: 39,577 miles (63,693 kilometers) Airports: 337 (235 paved) Ports & harbors: Chennai (Madras), Cochin, Jawaharlal Nehru, Kandla, Kolkata (Calcutta), Mumbai (Bombay), Vishakhapatnam

History at a Glance

500,000 B.C.	Evidence of early Stone Age people in what is now India.
9000–8000	Plant and animal domestication in Southwest Asia led to early agriculture.
2500	Indus River Civilization, irrigated agriculture and early communities.
1750	Migration of nomadic Aryans into northwest India.
1000	Early Hinduism.
500	Rise of Buddhism.
326	Alexander the Great invades.
324–184	Mauryan Empire expands across much of India.
200	Numerous invasions by tribes from the north and west.
320–550 A.D.	Gupta Dynasty dominates northern India.
455–528	Invasions by Huns from Central Asia; Gupta Empire destroyed.
997	Beginning of Muslim influence in India.
1192	Delhi Sultanate; Turkish and Afghan tribes begin a period of nearly four centuries of domination in northern India.
1498	Portuguese traders reach India.
1526–1858	Mughal Empire unifies northern and parts of southern India.
1757	East India Company gains control of Bengal and begins era of British influence in India.
1858	India becomes a British colony.
1920	Mahatma Gandhi begins campaign of peaceful civil disobedience.
1947	End of British rule; India becomes independent (dominantly Hindu) state; Pakistan created as a Muslim-majority state.
1948	Mahatma Gandhi assassinated by Hindu extremist.
1948	War with Pakistan over disputed territory of Kashmir.
1951–1952	Jawaharlal Nehru leads Congress Party to win in general elections.
1962	India loses border war with China.
1964	Death of Prime Minister Jawaharlal Nehru.
1965	Second war with Pakistan over Kashmir.
1966	Indira Gandhi, Nehru's daughter, becomes prime minister.
1971	War with Pakistan over creation of Bangladesh, formerly East Pakistan.

1984	Indira Gandhi is assassinated by Sikh bodyguards; followed in office by her son, Rajiv.
1990	Muslim separatist groups begin campaign of violence in Kashmir.
1991	Rajiv Gandhi assassinated.
1998	India conducts successful nuclear tests.
2000	India's population reaches one billion.
2002	A scientist and Muslim, Abdul Kalam, is elected President.

Further Reading

Basham, A. L. *The Wonder That Was India*. Sidgewick & Jackson, 2000.

Bayly, Susan. *Caste, Society, and Politics in India From the Eighteenth Century to the Modern Age (The New Cambridge History of India)*. Cambridge University Press, 2001.

Brown, Dale M. (Editor). *Ancient India: Land of Mystery*. Time-Life Books, 1995.

Cohen, Stephen Philip and Michael H. Armacost. *India: Emerging Power*. The Brookings Institution, 2001.

Collins, Larry, and Dominique Lapierre. *Freedom at Midnight*. Avon, 1983.

Das, Gurcharan. *India Unbound*. Knopf, 2001.

Dicks, Nicholas B. *Castes of Mind: Colonialism and the Making of Modern India*. Princeton University Press, 2001.

Jacobson, Doranne. *India: Land of Dreams and Fantasy*. Todtri Productions, 1992.

James, Lawrence. *Raj: The Making and Unmaking of British India*. Griffin Trade Paperback, 2000.

Keay, John. *India a History*. Grove Press, 2001.

Lapierre, Dominique. *City of Joy*. Warnerbooks, 1990.

McIntosh, Jane R. *A Peaceful Realm: The Rise and Fall of the Indus Civilization*. Westview Press, 2001.

Meadows, Peter (editor). *The Indus River: Biodiversity, Resources, Humankind*. Oxford University Press, 2002.

Metcalf, Barbara Daly, and Thomas R. Metcalf. *A Concise History of India*. Cambridge University Press, 2001.

Naipaul, V. S. *An Area of Darkness*. Vintage Books, 2002.

Nehru, Jawaharlal. *Discovery of India*. Oxford University Press, 1990.

Pandey, Gyanendra. *Remembering Partition: Violence, Nationalism and History in India*. Cambridge University Press, 2001.

Pinney, Christopher. *Camera Indica: The Social Life of Indian Photographs*. University of Chicago Press, 1998.

Srinivasan, Radhika. *Cultures of the World: India*. Marshall Cavendish, 1990.

Stein, Burton. *The New Cambridge History of India.* Cambridge University Press, 1989.

Tobias, Michael, Raghu Rai (Editor), and David Cohen (Editor). *A Day in the Life of India.* Collins Publishing, 1996.

Wild, Antony. *The East India Company: Trade and Conquest from 1600.* The Lyons Press, 2000.

Wolpert, Stanley A. *A New History of India.* Oxford University Press, 1999.

Wolpert, Stanley A. *Gandhi's Passion: The Life and Legacy of Mahatma Gandhi.* Oxford University Press, 2001.

Wolpert, Stanley A. *India.* University of California Press, 1991.

Index

Index

Picture Credits

About the Author

DOUGLAS A. PHILLIPS is a lifetime educator and writer who has worked and traveled in over 70 countries. During his career he has worked as a middle school teacher, as a curriculum developer, writer, and as a trainer of educators in various locations around the world. He has served as the President of the National Council for Geographic Education and has received the Outstanding Service Award from the National Council for the Social Studies along with numerous other awards. He, his wife Marlene, and their three children, Chris, Angela, and Daniel have lived in South Dakota and Alaska but he and his family now reside in Arizona where he writes and serves as an educational consultant. During his first visit to India he had an audience with Indira Gandhi and holds the country and its people close to his heart.

CHARLES F. ("FRITZ") GRITZNER is Distinguished Professor of Geography at South Dakota University in Brookings. He is now in his fifth decade of college teaching and research. During his career, he has taught more than 60 different courses, spanning the fields of physical, cultural, and regional geography. In addition to his teaching, he enjoys writing, working with teachers, and sharing his love for geography with students. As consulting editor for the MODERN WORLD NATIONS series, he has a wonderful opportunity to combine each of these "hobbies." Fritz has served as both president and executive director of the National Council for Geographic Education and has received the Council's highest honor, the George J. Miller Award for Distinguished Service.